PARTICIPANT OBSERVATION

PARTICIPANT OBSERVATION

James P. Spradley

Macalester College

HOLT, RINEHART AND WINSTON
New York   Chicago   San Francisco   Dallas
Montreal   Toronto   London   Sydney

Library of Congress Cataloging in Publication Data

Spradley, James P
  Participant observation.

  Bibliography: p. 183.
  Includes index.
  1. Participant observation. I. Title.
GN346.4.S68   301.2'07'23   79-17917
ISBN 0-03-044501-9

This book shows the beginning student how to do fieldwork using the method of *participant observation*. Anyone can follow the step-by-step instructions. You do not need a background in the social sciences. You will not need class lectures on research methods to supplement this book. It contains everything required to begin research, collect data, analyze what you find, and write up your report. All it takes is several hours each week and an interest in the adventure of fieldwork. In one semester you will begin and complete a qualitative research project. And in the process you will learn some things about social science that you could not acquire from this or any other book.

A quiet revolution has spread through the social sciences and many applied disciplines. A new appreciation for qualitative research has emerged among educators, urban planners, sociologists, nurses, psychologists, public interest lawyers, political scientists, and many others. There has come a profound realization that people everywhere have a way of life, a culture of their own, and if we want to understand humankind we must take these cultures seriously. Qualitative research—called *ethnography* by anthropologists—has come of age.

Like a stream that rises slowly, then spills over its banks, sending rivulets of water in many directions, the ethnographic revolution has overflowed the banks of anthropology. This stream had its beginning in fieldwork among the Trobriand Islanders off the coast of New Guinea, among the Eskimo and Kwakiutl Indians of North America, and among the Andaman Islanders in Southeast Asia, But, no longer relegated to exotic cultures in far-off places, ethnography has come home, to become a fundamental tool for understanding ourselves and the multicultural societies of the modern world.

Several miles from Macalester College, in St. Paul, Minnesota, where I teach, there is a blood bank, an institution that exists in every large city in the United States. One researcher set out to understand this blood bank using the tools of ethnography. She watched the students and unemployed old men coming to sell their blood. She observed nurses checking their arms, hooking them up to tubes and needles, and carrying bags of blood to a storage room. She herself gave blood and listened to the casual conversations that occurred. Over a period of months she learned the special language and culture of the blood bank, then described it from the participant's point of view (Kruft 1978). She was doing ethnography.

Across the Mississippi River, in the city of Minneapolis, lives a man whose arms and legs were paralyzed when he broke his neck in a trampoline accident. Technically called a quadriplegic, he spends much of his time in a wheelchair; although he works full time as a professional, he must depend on others for many of the things that most of us take for granted. A premed student in one of my classes became interested in the culture of "quads" and spent many hours interviewing this man. He also visited other quads who lived in nursing homes and slowly came to understand life from their point of view. He did fieldwork in another culture that had direct applicability to his chosen field of medicine (Devney 1974). He was doing ethnography.

Several years ago I became interested in alcoholism and the difficulties of treating the skid row alcoholic. Using the ethnographic approach, I set out to study men who had lived on skid row for many years. Listening, watching, and allowing these men to become my teachers, I discovered a complex culture that gave shape and meaning to the lives of men most people wrote off as "derelicts" (Spradley 1970). I was doing ethnography.

Since 1900, the number of elderly in the United States reaching retirement age has increased by more than 500 percent. Jacobs (1974) set out to understand a large retirement community of approximately 5600 members. He visited the town, went to the shops, participated in clubs and organizations, and spent many hours listening to these elderly people explain their way of life. He wanted to understand this community from the members' point of view. He was doing ethnography. Similar examples of contemporary ethnography could be drawn from all parts of the world.

The new surge of interest in qualitative investigation has given rise to two pressing needs. First, the urgent need to clarify the nature of ethnography. As scholars and students from many disciplines attempt to do ethnography, they usually bring their own disciplinary assumptions to this approach. In many cases, ethnography becomes confused with other types of qualitative and descriptive studies. Because interviewing and participant observation can be used for other forms of investigation, it has become necessary to make clear what is meant by *ethnographic interviewing* and *participant observation* that leads to an *ethnographic description*. In Part I of this book, I define ethnography, identify some of its underlying assumptions, and distinguish it from other investigative approaches. I also discuss the ethics of doing ethnography and some criteria for selecting strategic ethnographic research projects.

The growing excitement about ethnography in many disciplines has given rise to a second need: specific instructions for learning ethnographic research skills. Most ethnographers have learned the skills of their trade through the apprenticeship system or by themselves in a kind of on-the-job training while doing their first field research. This book is a response to the need for a systematic handbook for doing ethnography. With its companion volume, *The Ethnographic Interview* (Spradley 1979), I have tried to make explicit the basic concepts and skills needed for doing ethnography. I call the approach in both of these books the Developmental Research Sequence (D.R.S.) Method. My interest in this approach began from a rather simple observation: *some tasks are best accomplished before other tasks when doing ethnography*. Ethnographers cannot do everything at once, even though fieldwork sometimes appears to demand it. Both ethnographic interviewing and participant observation, whether done separately or in combination, involve a series of tasks best carried out in some kind of *sequence*. The ethnographer, for example, must locate a social situation and informants before doing interviews and participant observation. Some questions are best asked before others; observation and interviews must precede analysis of interview data. As I began to work with this idea of *sequenced tasks*, I found it was not only valuable for my own research but it also had special importance to students and professionals trying to learn the skills for doing ethnography. What has emerged over a twelve-year period is a procedure for *learning* as well as *doing* ethnography. In a real sense this book is thus designed both for beginners who want to learn to do ethnography and for professional ethnographers who will necessarily want to adapt the procedures to their own style of investigation.

Part Two of the book, "The Developmental Research Sequence," sets forth a series of twelve major tasks that are designed to guide the investigator from the starting point of "selecting a social situation" to the goal of "writing the ethnography." Each of these larger tasks is broken down into many smaller ones that simplify the work of asking ethnographic questions and making ethnographic analyses. Those interested in a more extensive discussion of the D.R.S. Method as well as how the use of that method has placed certain limits on this book should consult "Appendix A: The D.R.S. Method."

Ethnography is an exciting enterprise. It reveals what people think and shows us the cultural meanings they use daily. It is the one systematic approach in the social sciences that leads us into those separate realities which others have learned and which they use to make sense out of their worlds. In our complex society the need for understanding how other people see their experience has never been greater. Ethnography is a tool with great promise: It offers the educator a way of seeing schools through the eyes of students; health professionals the opportunity of seeing health and disease through the eyes of patients from a myriad of different backgrounds; those in the criminal justice system a chance to view the world through the eyes of those who are helped and victimized by that system; and counselors an opportunity to see the world from their clients' points of view.

Ethnography offers all of us the chance to step outside our narrow cultural backgrounds, to set aside our socially inherited ethnocentrism, if only for a brief period, and to apprehend the world from the viewpoint of other human beings who live by different meaning systems. Ethnography, as I understand it, is more than an exclusive tool of anthropologists in their study of exotic cultures. Rather, it is a pathway to understanding the cultural differences that make us what we are as human beings. Perhaps the most important force behind the quiet ethnographic revolution is the widespread realization that cultural diversity is one of the great gifts bestowed on the human species. It is my hope that this book will enable those who use it to more fully apprehend the nature of that cultural diversity.

J.P.S.

ACKNOWLEDGMENTS

Many people have contributed to the ideas developed in this book. I am especially grateful to hundreds of students, both graduate and undergraduate, who have taken my courses in ethnographic fieldwork during the past dozen years. They have taught me much about doing ethnography, and their experiences are reflected in much of this book. In particular I am grateful to Macalester College and the Department of Anthropology for allowing me the freedom to experiment with different styles of teaching and learning.

I originally developed many of the ideas developed in this book while teaching a course with my colleague Professor Jeffrey E. Nash, Department of Sociology, Macalester College. I am indebted to Professor Nash for ideas, long discussion of many topics in this book, and for allowing me to learn from his skills as a participant observer. His ability to transform every situation into a qualitative research laboratory and then translate his findings into descriptive studies is unique among the social scientists I know.

Many others have made comments on the manuscript or have contributed by comments and suggestions, including David McCurdy, Thomas Correll, Oswald Werner, Calvin Peters, Richard Furlow, George Spindler, David Boynton, Herman Makler, and Mary Lou Burket. In 1976-77, through a Chautauqua-type short course sponsored by the American Association for the Advancement of Science, I presented many of these ideas to professionals from the fields of anthropology, sociology, history, psychology, education, and political science. Many of them made use of this approach in their research and teaching and their ideas have helped refine and clarify what is presented here.

The most important contributions came from Barbara Spradley. As my wife and colleague, she listened to the development of all these ideas, offered many suggestions, and provided constant encouragement. Without her assistance this book would not have been possible.

Contents

Part One

ETHNOGRAPHIC RESEARCH

Ethnographic fieldwork is the hallmark of cultural anthropology. Whether in a jungle village in Peru or on the streets of New York, the anthropologist goes to where people live and "does fieldwork." This means participating in activities, asking questions, eating strange foods, learning a new language, watching ceremonies, taking fieldnotes, washing clothes, writing letters home, tracing out genealogies, observing play, interviewing informants, and hundreds of other things. This vast range of activities often obscures the nature of the most fundamental task of all fieldwork—doing ethnography.

Ethnography is the work of describing a culture. The central aim of ethnography is to understand another way of life from the native point of view. The goal of ethnography, as Malinowski put it, is "to grasp the native's point of view, his relation to life, to realize *his* vision of *his* world" (1922:25). Fieldwork, then, involves the disciplined study of what the world is like to people who have learned to see, hear, speak, think, and act in ways that are different. Rather than *studying people,* ethnography means *learning from people.* Consider the following illustration.

George Hicks set out, in 1965, to learn about another way of life, that of the mountain people in an Appalachian valley (1976). His goal was to discover their culture, to learn to see the world from their perspective. With his family he moved into Little Laurel Valley, his daughter attended the local school, and his wife became one of the local Girl Scout leaders. Hicks soon discovered that stores and storekeepers were at the center of the valley's communication system, providing the most important social arena for the entire valley. He learned this by watching what other people did, by following their example, and slowly becoming part of the groups that congregated daily in the stores. He writes:

At least once each day I would visit several stores in the valley, and sit in on the groups of gossiping men or, if the storekeeper happened to be alone, perhaps attempt to clear up puzzling points about kinship obligations. I found these hours, particularly those spent in the presence of the two or three excellent storytellers in the Little Laurel, thoroughly enjoyable. . . . At other times, I helped a number of local men gather corn or hay, build sheds, cut trees, pull and pack galax, and search for rich stands of huckleberries. When I needed aid in, for example, repairing frozen water pipes, it was readily and cheerfully provided (1976:3).

In order to discover the hidden principles of another way of life, the researcher must become a *student*. Storekeepers and storytellers and local farmers become *teachers*. Instead of studying the "climate," the "flora," and the "fauna" that made up the environment of this Appalachian valley, Hicks tried to discover how these mountain people defined and evaluated trees and galax and huckleberries. He did not attempt to describe social life in terms of what most Americans know about "marriage," "family," and "friendship"; instead he sought to discover how these mountain people identified relatives and friends. He tried to learn the obligations they felt toward kinsmen and discover how they felt about friends. Discovering the *insider's* view is a different species of knowledge from one that rests mainly on the outsider's view, even when the outsider is a trained social scientist.

Consider another example, this time from the perspective of a non-Western ethnographer. Imagine an Eskimo woman setting out to learn the culture of Macalester College. What would she, so well schooled in the rich heritage of Eskimo culture, have to do in order to understand the culture of Macalester College students, faculty, and staff? How would she discover the patterns that made up their lives? How would she avoid imposing Eskimo ideas, categories, and values on everything she saw?

First, and perhaps most difficult, she would have to set aside her belief in *naive realism,* the almost universal belief that all people define the *real* world of objects, events, and living creatures in pretty much the same way. Human languages may differ from one society to the next, but behind the strange words and sentences, all people are talking about the same things. The naive realist assumes that love, snow, marriage, worship, animals, death, food, and hundreds of other things have essentially the same meaning to all human beings. Although few of us would admit to such ethnocentrism, the assumption may unconsciously influence our research. Ethnography starts with a conscious attitude of almost complete ignorance. "I don't know how the people at Macalester College understand their world. That remains to be discovered."

This Eskimo woman would have to begin by learning the language spoken by students, faculty, and staff. She could stroll the campus paths, sit in classes, and attend special events, but only if she consciously tried to see things from the native point of view would she grasp their perspective. She would need to observe and listen to first-year students during their week-long orientation program. She would have to stand in line during registration, listen to students discuss the classes they hoped to get, and visit departments to watch faculty advising students on course selection. She would want to observe secretaries typing, janitors sweeping, and maintenance personnel plowing snow from walks. She would watch the more than 1600 students crowd into the post office area to open their tiny mailboxes, and she would listen to their comments about junk mail and letters from home and no mail at all. She would attend faculty meetings to watch what went on, recording what professors and administrators said and how they behaved. She would sample various courses, attend "keggers" on weekends, read the *Mac Weekly,* and listen by the hour to students discussing things like their "relationships," the "football team," and "work study." She would want to learn the *meanings* of all these things. She would have to listen to the members of this college community, watch what they did, and participate in their activities to learn such meanings.

The essential core of ethnography is this concern with the meaning of actions and events to the people we seek to understand. Some of these meanings are directly expressed in language; many are taken for granted and communicated only indirectly through word and action. But in every society people make constant use of these complex meaning systems to organize their behavior, to understand themselves and others, and to make sense out of the world in which they live. These systems of meaning constitute their culture; ethnography always implies a theory of culture.

CULTURE

When ethnographers study other cultures, they must deal with three fundamental aspects of human experience: what people do, what people know, and the things people make and use. When each of these are learned and shared by members of some group, we speak of them as *cultural behavior, cultural knowledge,* and *cultural artifacts.* Whenever you do ethnographic fieldwork, you will want to distinguish among these three, although in most situations they are usually mixed together. Let's try to unravel them.

Recently I took a commuter train from a western suburb to downtown Chicago. It was late in the day, and when I boarded the train only a handful of people were scattered about the car. Each was engaged in a common form of *cultural behavior: reading.* Across the aisle a man held the *Chicago Tribune* out in front of him, looking intently at the small print and every now and then turning the pages noisily. In front of him a young woman held a paperback book about twelve inches from her face. I could see her head shift slightly as her eyes moved from the bottom of one page to the top of the next. Near the front of the car a student was reading a large textbook and using a pen to underline words and sentences. Directly in front of me I noticed a man looking at the ticket he had purchased and reading it. It took me an instant to survey this scene and then I settled back, looked out the window, and read a billboard advertisement for a plumbing servce proclaiming it would open any plugged drains. All of us were engaged in the same kind of cultural behavior: reading.

This common activity depended on a great many *cultural artifacts,* the things people shape or make from natural resources. I could see artifacts like books and tickets and newspapers and billboards, all of which contained tiny black marks arranged into intricate patterns called "letters." And these tiny artifacts were arranged into larger patterns of words, sentences, and paragraphs. Those of us on that commuter train could read, in part, because of still other artifacts: the bark of trees made into paper; steel made into printing presses; dyes of various colors made into ink; glue used to hold book pages together; large wooden frames to hold billboards. If an ethnographer wanted to understand the full cultural meaning of reading in our society, it would involve a careful study of these and many other cultural artifacts.

Although we can easily see behavior and artifacts, they represent only the thin surface of a deep lake. Beneath the surface, hidden from view, lies a vast reservoir of *cultural knowledge*. Think for a moment what the people on that train needed to know in order to read. First, they had to know the grammatical rules for at least one language. Then they had to learn what all the little marks on paper represented. They also had to know the meaning of space and lines and pages. They had learned cultural rules like "move your eyes from left to right, from the top of the page to the bottom." They had to know that a sentence at the bottom of a page continues on the top of the next page. The man reading a newspaper had to know a great deal about columns and the spaces between columns and what headlines mean. All of us needed to know what kinds of messages were intended by whoever wrote what we read. If a person cannot distinguish the importance of a message on a billboard from one that comes in a letter from a spouse or child, problems would develop. I knew how to recognize when other people were reading. We all knew it was impolite to read aloud on a train. We all knew how to feel when reading things like jokes or calamitous news in the paper. Our culture has a large body of shared knowledge that people learn and use to engage in this behavior called *reading* and make proper use of the artifacts connected with it.

Although cultural knowledge is hidden from view, it is of fundamental importance because we all use it constantly to generate behavior and interpret our experience. Cultural knowledge is so important that I will frequently use the broader term *culture* when speaking about it. Indeed, I will define culture as *the acquired knowledge people use to interpret experience and generate behavior*. Let's consider another example to see how people use their culture to interpret experience and do things.

One afternoon in 1973 I came across the following news item in the *Minneapolis Tribune:*

CROWD MISTAKES RESCUE ATTEMPT, ATTACKS POLICE

Nov. 23, 1973. Hartford, Connecticut. Three policemen giving a heart massage and oxygen to a heart attack victim Friday were attacked by a crowd of 75 to 100 persons who apparently did not realize what the policemen were doing.

Other policemen fended off the crowd of mostly Spanish-speaking residents until an ambulance arrived. Police said they tried to explain to the crowd what they were doing, but the crowd apparently thought they were beating the woman.

Despite the policemen's efforts the victim, Evangelica Echevacria, 59, died.

Here we see people using their culture. Members of two different groups observed the same event but their *interpretations* were drastically different. The crowd used their cultural knowledge (a) to interpret the behavior of the policemen as cruel and (b) to act on the woman's behalf to put a stop to what they perceived as brutality. They had acquired the cultural principles for acting and interpreting things in this way through a particular shared experience.

The policemen, on the other hand, used their cultural knowledge (a) to interpret the woman's condition as heart failure and their own behavior as a life-saving effort and (b) to give her cardiac massage and oxygen. They used artifacts like an oxygen mask and an ambulance. Furthermore, they interpreted the actions of the crowd in an entirely different manner from how the crowd saw their own behavior. The two groups of people each had elaborate cultural rules for interpreting their experience and for acting in emergency situations, and the conflict arose, at least in part, because these cultural rules were so different.

We can now diagram this definition of culture and see more clearly the relationships among knowledge, behavior, and artifacts (Figure 1). By identifying cultural knowledge as fundamental, we have merely shifted the emphasis from behavior and artifacts to their *meaning*. The ethnographer observes behavior but goes beyond it to inquire about the meaning of that behavior. The ethnographer sees artifacts and natural objects but goes beyond them to discover what meanings people assign to these objects. The ethnographer observes and records emotional states but goes beyond them to discover the meaning of fear, anxiety, anger, and other feelings.

As represented in Figure 1, cultural knowledge exists at two levels of consciousness. *Explicit culture* makes up part of what we know, a level of knowledge people can communicate about with relative ease. When George Hicks asked storekeepers and others in Little Laurel Valley about their relatives, he discovered that any adult over fifty could tell him the genealogical connections among large numbers of people. They knew how to trace kin relationships and the cultural rules for appropriate behavior among kinsmen. All of us have acquired large areas of cultural knowledge such as this which we can talk about and make explicit.

At the same time, a large portion of our cultural knowledge remains *tacit*, outside our awareness. Edward Hall has done much to elucidate the nature of tacit cultural knowledge in his books *The Silent Language* (1959) and *The Hidden Dimension* (1966). The way each culture defines space often occurs at the level of tacit knowledge. Hall points out that all of us have acquired

7

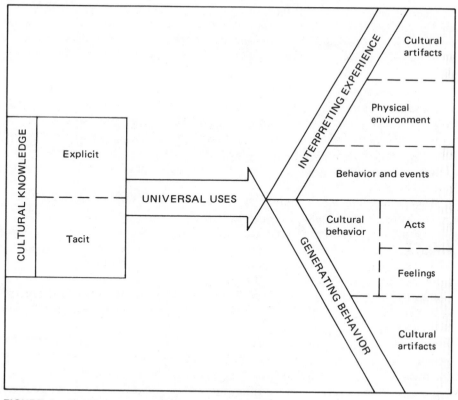

FIGURE 1. The Two Levels of Cultural Knowledge

thousands of spatial cues about how close to stand to others, how to arrange furniture, when to touch others, and when to feel cramped inside of a room. Without realizing that our tacit culture is operating, we begin to feel uneasy when someone from another culture stands too close, breathes on us when talking, touches us, or when we find furniture arranged in the center of the room rather than around the edges. Ethnography is the study of both explicit and tacit cultural knowledge; the research strategies discussed in this book are designed to reveal both levels.

The concept of culture as acquired knowledge has much in common with symbolic interactionism, a theory that seeks to explain human behavior in terms of meanings. Symbolic interactionism has its roots in the work of sociologists like Cooley, Mead, and Thomas (Manis and Meltzer 1967). Blumer has identified three premises on which this theory rests (1969).

The first premise is that "human beings act toward things on the basis of the meanings that the things have for them" (1969:2). The policemen and the crowd in our earlier example interacted on the basis of the meanings things had for them. The geographic location, the types of people, the police car, the policemen's movements, the sick woman's behavior, and the activities of the onlookers—all were *symbols* with special meanings. People did not act toward the things themselves, but to their meanings.

The second premise underlying symbolic interactionism is that the "meaning of such things is derived from, or arise out of, the social interaction that on has with one's fellows" (Blumer 1969:2). Culture, as a shared system of meanings, is learned, revised, maintained, and defined in the context of people interacting. The crowd came to share their definitions of police behavior through interacting with one another and through past associations with the police. The police officers acquired the cultural meanings they used through interacting with other officers and members of the community. The culture of each group was inextricably bound up with the social life of their particular communities.

The third premise of symbolic interactionism is that "meanings are handled in, and modified through, an interpretive process used by the person dealing with the things he encounters" (Blumer 1969:2). Neither the crowd nor the policemen were automatons, driven by their culture to act in the way they did. Rather, they used their cultural knowledge to interpret and evaluate the situation. At any moment, a member of the crowd might have interpreted the behavior of the policemen in a slightly different way, leading to a different reaction.

We may see this interpretive aspect more clearly if we think of culture as a cognitive map. In the recurrent activities that make up everyday life, we refer to this map. It serves as a guide for acting and for interpreting our experience; it does not compel us to follow a particular course. Like this brief drama between the policemen, a dying woman, and the crowd, much of life is a series of unanticipated social occasions. Although our culture may not include a detailed map for such occasions, it does provide principles for interpreting and responding to them. Rather than a rigid map that people must follow, culture is best thought of as

a set of principles for creating dramas, for writing script, and of course, for recruiting players and audiences. . . . Culture is not simply a cognitive map that people acquire, in whole or in part, more or less accurately, and then learn to read. People are not just map-readers; they are map-makers. People are cast out into imperfectly charted, continually revised sketch maps. Culture does not provide a cognitive map, but rather a set of principles for map making and navigation. Different cultures are like different schools of navigation designed to cope with different terrains and seas (Frake 1977:6–7).

If we take *meaning* seriously, as symbolic interactionists argue we must, it becomes necessary to study meaning carefully. We need a theory of meaning and a specific methodology designed for the investigation of it. This book presents such a theory and methodology.

MAKING CULTURAL INFERENCES

Culture, the knowledge that people have learned as members of a group, cannot be observed directly. In his study of glider pilots, for example, Rybski (1974) observed pilots at the airport and in their gliders, watching them take off, maneuver, and land. But only by "getting inside their heads" could he find out what flying meant to these glider pilots. If we want to find out what people know, we must get inside their heads. Although difficult, "this should not be an impossible feat: our subjects themselves accomplished it when they learned their culture and became 'native actors.' They had no mysterious avenues of perception not available to us as investigators" (Frake 1964a:133).

People everywhere learn their culture by making inferences. We generally use three types of information to make cultural inferences. We observe what people do (cultural behavior); we observe things people make and use such as clothes and tools (cultural artifacts); and we listen to what people say (speech messages). Every ethnographer employs this same process of inference to go beyond what is seen and heard to find out what people know. Making inferences involves reasoning from evidence (what we perceive) or from premises (what we assume). Children acquire their culture by watching and listening to adults and then making inferences about the cultural rules for behavior; with the acquisition of language, the learning accelerates. Whenever we are in a new situation we have to make inferences about what people know. An American student studying in a European country observed all the other students in a class immediately rise to their feet when the professor entered the room. She made an inference—"standing recognizes the authority or position of the teacher." Later, the students explained further to her the importance of standing when a professor entered the class and gave reasons for doing it. Through what they said she made additional inferences about their cultural knowledge.

In doing fieldwork, you will constantly be making cultural inferences from what people say, from the way they act, and from the artifacts they use. At first, each cultural inference is only a hypothesis about what people know. These hypotheses must be tested over and over again until the ethnographer becomes relatively certain that people share a particular system of cultural meanings. None of the sources for making inferences—behavior, speech, artifacts—are fool-proof, but together they can lead to an adequate cultural description. And we can evaluate the adequacy of the description "by the ability of a stranger to the culture (who may be the ethnographer) to use the ethnographer's statements as instructions for appropriately anticipating the scenes of the society" (Frake 1964b:112). (See Figure 2.)

Sometimes cultural knowledge is communicated by language in such a direct manner that we can make inferences with great ease. Instructions to children such as "wash your hands before dinner" and "don't go swimming

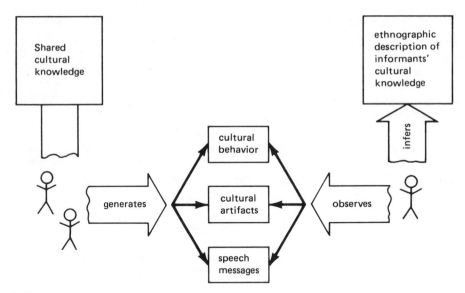

FIGURE 2. Making Cultural Inferences

after you eat or you'll get cramps" are representative expressions of such *explicit cultural knowledge*. In his study of glider pilots, Rybski (1947) learned from informants that the flying they did was called "soaring" and involved three distinct forms: *ridge soaring, wave soaring,* and *thermalling.* Informants could talk easily about this cultural knowledge. It is important to point out that studying explicit culture through the way people talk does not eliminate the need for making inferences. It only makes the task less difficult.

However, as I said earlier, a large part of any culture consists of *tacit knowledge*. Informants always know things they cannot talk about or express in direct ways. The ethnographer must then make inferences about what people know by listening carefully to what they say, by observing their behavior, and by studying artifacts and their use. With reference to discovering tacit cultural knowledge, Malinowski wrote:

The native takes his fundamental assumptions for granted, and if he reasons or inquires into matters of belief, it would be always in regard to details and concrete applications. Any attempts on the part of the ethnographer to induce his informant to formulate such a general statement would have to be in the form of leading questions of the worst type because in these leading questions he would have to introduce words and concepts essentially foreign to the native. Once the informant grasped their meaning, his outlook would be warped by our own ideas having been poured into it. Thus, the ethnographer must draw the generalizations for himself, must formulate the abstract statement without the direct help of a native informant (1950:396).

11

Every ethnographer makes use of what people say in seeking to describe their culture. Both explicit and tacit cultural knowledge are revealed through speech, whether in casual comments or lengthy interviews. Because language is the primary means for transmitting culture from one generation to the next, much of any culture is encoded in linguistic form. In the companion volume, *The Ethnographic Interview* (1979), I have focused exclusively on making inferences from what people say. In this book (*Participant Observation*), I have focused more on making inferences from what people do (cultural behavior) and what they make and use (cultural artifacts). Because every ethnographer who does participant observation will record things people say, I have also included some discussion of making inferences from what they say (speech messages).

Ethnography is a culture-studying culture. It consists of a body of knowledge that includes research techniques, ethnographic theory, and hundreds of cultural descriptions. It seeks to build a systematic understanding of all human cultures from the perspectives of those who have learned them. Ethnography is based on an assumption that warrants careful examination: knowledge of all cultures is valuable. To what end does the ethnographer collect information? For what reasons do we try to find out what people have to know to traverse the polar cap on dog sled, live in remote Melanesian villages, or work in New York skyscrapers? Why should anyone do ethnography?

UNDERSTANDING THE HUMAN SPECIES

Let's begin with the goal of scientific anthropology: to describe and explain the regularities and variations in social behavior. Perhaps the most striking feature of human beings is their diversity. Why does a single species exhibit such variation, creating different marriage patterns, holding different values, eating different foods, rearing children in different ways, believing in different gods, and pursuing different goals? If we are to understand this diversity, we must begin by carefully describing it. Most of the diversity in the human species results from the cultures each human group has created and passed on from one generation to the next. Cultural description, the central task of ethnography, is the first step in understanding the human species.

It is one thing to describe differences, another to account for them. Explanation of cultural differences depends, in part, on making cross-cultural comparisons, but this task, in turn, depends on adequate ethnographic studies. Much of the comparative work in anthropology has been hampered by shoddy ethnographies, often caused by investigations that impose Western concepts onto non-Western cultures, thereby distorting the results. Comparison not only reveals differences but also similarities, what is common among all cultures of the world. In the most general sense, then, ethnography contributes directly to both description and explanation of regularities and variations in human social behavior.

Many of the social sciences have more limited objectives. In any study of human behavior ethnography has an important role to play. We can identify several specific contributions.

Informing Culture-Bound Theories

Each culture provides people with a way of seeing the world, by categorizing, encoding, and otherwise defining the world in which they live. Culture includes assumptions about the nature of reality as well as specific information about that reality. It includes values that specify the good, the true, and the believable. Whenever people learn a culture, they are to some extent imprisoned without knowing it. Anthropologists speak of this mode of existence as being "culture-bound," that is, living inside of a particular reality that is taken for granted as "the reality."

Social scientists and their theories are no less culture-bound than other human beings. Western educational systems infuse all of us with ways of interpreting experience. Tacit assumptions about the world find their way into the theories of every academic discipline—literary criticism, physical science, history, and all of the social sciences. Ethnography alone seeks to document the existence of *alternative* realities and to describe these realities in their own terms. Thus, it can provide a corrective for theories that arise in Western social science.

Take, for example, the theory of cultural deprivation, an idea that arose in concrete form in the United States during the 1960s to explain the educational failure of many children. In order to account for their lack of achievement, it was proposed that they were "culturally deprived." Studies of cultural deprivation were undertaken, mostly focusing on Indians, blacks, chicanos, and other cultural groups. This theory can be confirmed by studying children from these cultures through the theory's protective screen. However, ethnographic research on the cultures of so-called culturally deprived children reveals a different story. They have elaborate, sophisticated, and adaptive cultures that are simply different from the ones espoused by the educational system. Although still supported in some quarters, this theory is culture-bound. Cultural deprivation is merely a way of saying that people are deprived of "my culture." Certainly no one would argue that such children do not speak adequate Spanish or Black English, that they do not do well the things that are considered rewarding in *their* cultures. But the culture-bound nature of psychological and sociological theories extends far beyond notions of cultural deprivation. All theories developed in Western behavioral science are based on tacit premises of Western culture, usually the middle-class version most typical of professionals.

Ethnography in itself does not escape being culture-bound. However, it provides descriptions that reveal the range of explanatory models created by human beings. It can serve as a beacon that shows the culture-bound nature of social science theories. It says to all investigators of human behavior, "Before you impose your theories on the people you study, find out how those people define the world." Ethnography can describe in detail the folk theories that have been tested in actual living situations over generations of time. And as we come to understand personality, society, individuals, and environments from the perspective of other than the professional scientific cultures, it will lead to a sense of epistemological humility; as we become aware of the tentative nature of our theories, we are thus able to revise them to be less ethnocentric.

Discovering Grounded Theory

Much social science research has been directed toward the task of *testing* formal theories. One alternative to such theories, and a strategy that reduces ethnocentrism, is the development of theories grounded in empirical data of cultural description, what Glaser and Strauss (1967) have called "grounded theory." Ethnography offers an excellent strategy for discovering grounded theory. For example, an ethnography of successful school children from minority cultures in the United States could develop grounded theories about school performance. One such study revealed that, rather than being culturally deprived, such children are *culturally overwhelmed,* that success in school performance required the capacity to become *bicultural.* But grounded theory can be developed in any substantive area of human experience. Personality theories can be informed by careful ethnographies of folk medical theories. Decision-making theory can be informed by first discovering the cultural rules for decision-making in a particular organization. The list could go on and on, for almost every area of social science theory has its counterpart in the taken-for-granted cultures of the world.

Understanding Complex Societies

Until recently, ethnography was largely relegated to small, non-Western cultures. The value of studying these societies was readily accepted—after all, we didn't know much about them and we couldn't conduct surveys or experiments, so ethnography seemed appropriate. However, the value of ethnography in understanding our own society was often overlooked.

Our culture has imposed on us a myth about our complex society—the myth of the melting pot. Social scientists have talked about "American culture" as if it included a set of values shared by everyone living in the United States. It has become increasingly clear that our culture is not homogeneous, that people who live in modern, complex societies actually live by many different cultural codes. Not only is this true of the most obvious ethnic groups but each occupation group also exhibits cultural differences. Our schools have their own cultural systems, and even within the same institution people see things differently. Consider the language, values, clothing styles, and activities of high school students in contrast to high school teachers and staff. The difference in their cultures is striking, yet often ignored. Guards and prisoners in jails, patients and physicians in hospitals, the elderly, the various religious groups—all have cultural perspectives. The physically handicapped live in a different world from those not handicapped even though they live in the same town. As people move from one cultural scene to another in complex societies, they employ different cultural rules. Ethnography offers one of the best ways to understand these complex features of modern life. It can show the range of cultural differences and how people with diverse perspectives interact.

Understanding Human Behavior

Human behavior, in contrast to animal behavior, has meanings to the actor, meanings that can be discovered. We can ask a person collecting seashells about her actions, what she is doing, why she is doing it. Even when people participate in carefully contrived scientific experiments, they define the experiment and their involvement in it. And these definitions are always influenced by specific cultural backgrounds. Any explanation of behavior which excludes what the actors themselves know, how they define their actions, remains a partial explanation that distorts the human situation. The tools of ethnography offer one means to deal with this fact of meaning.

One end of ethnography, then, is to understand the human species. Ethnography yields empirical data about the lives of people in specific situations. It allows us to see alternative realities and modify our culture-bound theories of human behavior. But is knowledge for understanding, even scientific understanding, enough? I believe it is not. However, ethnography offers other dividends to anyone involved in culture change, social planning, or trying to solve a wide range of human problems.

ETHNOGRAPHY IN THE SERVICE OF HUMANKIND

There was a time when "knowledge for knowledge's sake" was sufficient reason for doing social science, at least for those who believed in the inevitability of progress and the inherent goodness of science. But that time has long since passed. One reason lies in the changes in the human situation:

In the last few decades, mankind has been overcome by the most change in its entire history. Modern science and technology have created so close a network of communication, transport, economic interdependence—and potential nuclear destruction—that planet earth, on its journey through infinity, has acquired the intimacy, the fellowship, and the vulnerability of a spaceship (Ward, 1966:vii).

That vulnerability makes our responsibility clearer if not easier. To ignore this vulnerability is like astronauts studying the effects of boredom and weightlessness on fellow astronauts while the spaceship runs out of oxygen, exhausts its fuel supply, and the crew verges on mutiny.

In addition, scientists can no longer ignore the uses to which research findings are put. This applies not only to research in genetics and atomic energy but also to ethnographic studies. Cultural descriptions can be used to oppress people or to set them free. I know of one case in which the South African government used ethnographic descriptions to make its apartheid policy more effective. I knew that my own descriptions of the culture of skid row drunks could be used by police departments to more easily arrest these men. That knowledge placed a special responsibility on me regarding where and when to publish the ethnography. In our world-become-spaceship where knowledge is power, ethnographers must consider the potential uses of their research.

In spite of these facts, some people continue to maintain that scientists need not concern themselves with the practical relevance of their research, a view that is deeply rooted in the academic value system. More than forty years ago, in his classic book *Knowledge for What?*, Robert Lynd described the dichotomy.

The time outlooks of the scholar-scientist and of the practical men of affairs who surround the world of science tend to be different. The former works in a long, leisurely world in which the hands of the clock crawl slowly over a vast dial; to him, the precise penetration of the unknown seems too grand an enterprise to be hurried, and one simply works ahead within study walls relatively sound-proofed against the clamorous urgencies of the world outside. In this time-universe of the scholar-scientist certain supporting assumptions have grown up such as "impersonal objectivity," "aloofness from the strife of rival values," and the self-justifying goodness of "new knowledge" about anything, big or little. . . . The practical man of affairs, on the other hand, works by a small time-dial over which the second-hand of immediacy hurries incessantly. "Never mind the long past and the infinite future," insists the clattering little monitor, "but do this, fix this—now, before tomorrow morning." It has been taken for granted, in general, that there is no need to synchronize the two time-worlds of the scholar-scientist and of the practical man. Immediate relevance has not been regarded as so important as ultimate relevance; and, in the burgeoning nineteenth-century world which viewed all time as moving within the Master System of Progress, there was seemingly large justification for this optimistic tolerance (1939:1–2).

One force at work today that makes it imperative for ethnographers to synchronize these two perspectives comes from the people we study. In many places we can no longer collect cultural information from people merely to fill the bank of scientific knowledge. Informants are asking, even demanding, "Ethnography for what? Do you want to study our culture to build your theories of poverty? Can't you see that our children go hungry? Do you want to study folk beliefs about water witching? What about the new nuclear power plant that contaminates our drinking water with radioactive wastes? Do you want to study kinship terms to build ever more esoteric theories? What about our elderly kinsmen who live in poverty and loneliness? Do you want to study our schools to propose new theories of learning? Our most pressing need is for schools that serve our children's needs in the language they understand."

One way to synchronize the needs of people and the goals of ethnography is to consult with informants to determine urgent research topics. Instead of beginning with theoretical problems, the ethnographer can begin with informant-expressed needs, then develop a research agenda to relate these topics to the enduring concerns within social science. Surely the needs of informants should have equal weight with "scientific interest" in setting ethnographic priorities. More often than not, informants can identify urgent research more clearly than the ethnographer. In my own study of skid row men (Spradley 1970), for example, I began with an interest in the social structure of an alcoholism treatment center. My informants, longtime drunks who were spending life sentences on the installment plan in the Seattle city jail, suggested more urgent research possibilities. "Why don't you study what goes on in that jail?" they would ask. And so I shifted my goals to studying the culture of the jail, the social structure of inmates, and how drunks were oppressed by the jail system. My theoretical and scholarly interests could have been served by either project; the needs of tramps were best served by studying the oppression they experienced in jail.

Another way to synchronize human needs with the accumulation of scientific knowledge is through what I call "strategic research." Instead of beginning ethnographic projects from an interest in some particular culture, area of the world, or theoretical concern, strategic research begins with an interest in human problems. These problems suggest needed changes and information needed to make such changes. For example, in a discussion on strategies for revitalizing American culture, I suggested the following priorities for strategic research (Spradley 1976a:111):

1. A health care system that provides adequate care for all members of the society.
2. The provision of economic resources for all people sufficient to eliminate poverty and provided in a way that does not destroy the privacy and dignity of any recipient.
3. Equal rights and opportunities for all classes of citizens, including women, blacks, native Americans, chicanos, the elderly, children, and others.
4. Public institutions, such as schools, courts, and governments, that are designed for a multicultural constituency.
5. Socially responsible corporations that operate in the public interest as well as in the private interest.
6. Zero population growth.

7. An ecologically balanced economy based on recycling and responsible for the protection of natural resources.
8. Education for all people, at every stage of life, that equips them to cope with the complexity of choice in our rapidly changing society.
9. Work roles and environments that contribute directly to the workers' sense of meaning and purpose in life.
10. Opportunity for alternative career patterns and more flexible life-cycle sequencing with multiple involvement for youth, retired persons, and the elderly.

After identifying a general area such as an adequate health care system, strategic research translates that identification into a specific research project, which can then lead to consultation with informants and a strategic project. For example, anthropologist Oswald Werner, of Northwestern University, has been conducting ethnographic research among the Navaho for many years. In consultation with informants and out of a concern for adequate medical care for the Navaho, he selected a strategic research project: the development of an encyclopedia of Navaho medical knowledge, of which three volumes in a ten-volume cultural description have been completed. The project has many immediate uses both in preserving Navaho medical knowledge and also in adapting Western medicine for the most effective use among the Navaho. As Navaho healers and Western health professionals increasingly work together, there is an urgent need for each to understand the medical knowledge of the other. Ethnographic research, in this case, is serving both the needs of the Navaho in solving pressing health problems and also the accumulation of theoretically important information for understanding human behavior.

Consider the priority identified above for "socially responsible corporations that operate in the public interest as well as in the private interest." This need suggests hundreds of strategic ethnographic research projects. We need to know how decisions are made in corporate board rooms, something that could be discovered through ethnography. We need to know how lobbying efforts of corporations affect every state legislature, in short an ethnography of corporate lobbying. We need to know how corporations bypass laws enacted to control them. As some corporations change to act more and more in the public interest, we need ethnographic descriptions of their efforts to serve as models for others. In short, we need extensive ethnographic research to understand this form of social organization in our own society and to know the extent to which corporations affect all our interests.

Ethnography for what? For understanding the human species but also for serving the needs of humankind. One of the great challenges facing every ethnographer is the synchronization of these two uses of research. If we recognize that ethnography can be done to serve the needs of informants as well as ethnographer, we come face-to-face with the *ethical* dimension of research. Every ethnographer, whether student or professional, must consider a number of ethical issues in doing fieldwork.

ETHICAL PRINCIPLES

Informants are human beings with problems, concerns, and interests. The values held by any particular ethnographer do not always coincide with those held by informants. In doing fieldwork one is always faced with conflicting values and a wide range of possible choices. Should I tape record what an informant says or merely make a written record? How will I use the data collected and should I tell informants how it will be used? Should I study the kinship terms used by informants or the tactics used by the colonial government to keep them oppressed? If I observe someone who engages in illegal behavior, should I make my field notes inaccessible to the police? If informants are children, should teachers or parents have access to my fieldnotes? Whenever faced by choices such as these, the decision will necessarily involve an appeal to some set of ethical principles based on underlying values.

In 1971, the Council of the American Anthropological Association adopted a set of principles to guide ethnographers when faced with conflicting choices. These *Principles of Professional Responsibility* begin with the following preamble:

Anthropologists work in many parts of the world in close personal association with the peoples and situations they study. Their professional situation is, therefore, uniquely varied and complex. They are involved with their discipline, their colleagues, their students, their sponsors, their subjects, their own and host governments, the particular individuals and groups with whom they do their fieldwork, other populations and interest groups in the nations within which they work, and the study of processes and issues affecting general human welfare. In a field of such complex involvements, misunderstandings, conflicts, and the necessity to make choices among conflicting values are bound to arise and to generate ethical dilemmas. It is a prime responsibility of anthropologists to anticipate these and to plan to resolve them in such a way as to do damage neither to those whom they study nor, in so far as possible, to their scholarly community. Where these conditions cannot be met, the anthropologist would be well-advised not to pursue the particular piece of research.

The great variation and complexity of fieldwork situations make it difficult, if not impossible, to adopt a single set of standards for all ethnographers. However, the following ethical principles, which are based on those adopted by the American Anthropological Association, can serve as a useful guide.

Consider Informants First

In research, an anthropologist's paramount responsibility is to those he studies. When there is a conflict of interest, these individuals must come first. The anthropologist must do everything within his power to protect their physical, social, and psychological welfare and to honor their dignity and privacy.

(Principles of Professional Responsibility, 1971, para. 1)

Ethnographic research often involves more than ethnographers and informants. Sponsors may provide funds for the support of research, or gatekeepers may have the power to give or withhold permission to conduct interviews and make observations. In complex societies, informants' lives are frequently intertwined with the lives of other people. For example, in studying cocktail waitresses, Spradley and Mann (1975) discovered that the bartenders, customers, and owners of the bar all had certain interests, often in conflict with those of the waitresses. Tramps were constantly involved with treatment center staff, policemen, and county health officials (Spradley 1970). The ethnographer cannot assume that informants' interests are the same as those of other people. All ethnography must include inquiries to discover the interests and concerns of informants, and when choices are made, these interests must be considered first.

Safeguard Informants' Rights, Interests, and Sensitivities

Where research involves the acquisition of material and information transferred on the assumption of trust between persons, it is axiomatic that the rights, interests, and sensitivities of those studied must be safeguarded.

(Principles of Professional Responsibility, para. 1,a)

This principle suggests that ethnographers go beyond merely *considering* the interests of informants. We have a positive responsibility to *safeguard* their rights, their interests, and even their sensitivities. We must examine the implications of our research from this vantage point, for it may have consequences unseen by informants.

James Sewid, a Kwakiutl Indian in British Columbia, was an excellent informant, and together we recorded his life history about growing up during the early part of this century (Spradley 1969). When it became apparent that the edited transcripts might become a published book, I decided to safeguard Mr. Sewid's rights by making him a full partner who signed the contract with Yale University Press. He shared equally in all royalties and had the right to decide, with me, on crucial matters of content. I also wanted to safeguard his sensitivities, so before we submitted the final manuscript I read the completed version to both him and his wife. They made deletions and changes that were in their best interests, changes that reflected their sensitivities, not mine.

No matter how unobtrusive, ethnographic research always pries into the lives of informants. Participant observation represents a powerful tool for invading other people's way of life. It reveals information that can be used to *affirm* their rights, interests, and sensitivities or to *violate* them. All informants must have the protection of saying things "off the record" that never find their way into the ethnographer's fieldnotes.

Communicate Research Objectives

The aims of the investigation should be communicated as well as possible to the informant.

(*Principles of Professional Responsibility*, 1971, para. 1,b)

Informants have a right to know the ethnographer's aims. This does not require a full course on the nature of ethnography. The scholar's aims can often be explained simply: "I want to understand what life at Brady's Bar is like from your perspective as a cocktail waitress. I think this will help us to understand the role of women who work in this type of job. I'll be writing up my study as a description of the role of cocktail waitresses."

Communicating the aims of research must often become a process of unfolding rather than a once-and-for-all declaration. The ethnographer must decide to whom the aims will be explained. Certainly anyone who participates in ethnographic interviews deserves an explanation. In our study of Brady's Bar we explained our goals to the cocktail waitresses; our study focused on their role. We did not talk with all the customers and all the bartenders, although their behavior certainly entered into our study. In this particular study, communicating the aims was made more difficult because one of the researchers assumed the role of cocktail waitress and had difficulty convincing others to take her role as researcher seriously. In a detailed analysis of that role, Mann (1976) has discussed the ethical problems connected with communicating the aims of research.

For the beginning ethnographer, especially those who are students, the primary aim may be to learn how to study another culture. One might communicate this goal quite simply: "I want to find out what it's like to be a student in the fourth grade. As a university student myself, I'm learning how to observe and discover things from your point of view. I'll be writing a paper on what you and other children in this fourth-grade classroom do each day, the things you like best, and just what it's like to be in the fourth grade."

However, as discussed in the last chapter, the aims of research often need to go beyond the mere accumulation of knowledge. Every ethnographic research project should, to some extent, include a dialogue with informants to explore ways in which the study can be useful to informants. The *Principles of Professional Responsibility* include a specific statement in this regard (para. 1,h): "Every effort should be exerted to cooperate with members of the host society in the planning and execution of research projects." This means planning not only with teachers and administrators, if one is studying a fourth-grade classroom for instance, but also with the students. In many cases, since informants do not yet understand the nature of ethnography, the aims of research will have to develop during the study. This means the ethnographer, in consultation with informants, must be willing to direct the investigation into paths suggested by informants. I began my research with skid row tramps by explaining, "I want to understand alcoholism from the perspective of men like yourself who are repeatedly arrested for being drunk." But as I progressed, informants' interests led to a change in goals. I communicated my new aims to each informant I interviewed, explaining that my investigation of life in jail could perhaps improve conditions there for incarcerated alcoholics.

The more intimately one works with informants, the more important becomes the task of communicating the aims of research. In doing participant observation without interviewing or intimate contact, however, especially in public places, one may not need to communicate the aims of research. For example, if you decide to study the cultural rules for riding city busses, you can participate in the normal activities of bus riding without asking permissions and without revealing your research goals to anyone. You have chosen a public place; in our society anyone has the right to observe what others are doing in public and to make cultural inferences about patterns of behavior. Furthermore, it would be virtually impossible to inform all the people you see on the busses about your research. However, observing in public places does not eliminate the need to protect the privacy of the people one studies when writing up ethnographic descriptions.

Protect the Privacy of Informants

Informants have a right to remain anonymous. This right should be respected both where it has been promised explicitly and where no clear understanding to the contrary has been reached. These strictures apply to the collection of data by means of cameras, tape recorders, and other data-gathering devices, as well as to data collected in face-to-face interviews or in participant observation. Those being studied should understand the capacities of such devices; they should be free to reject them if they wish; and if they accept them, the results obtained should be consonant with the informant's right to welfare, dignity and privacy. Despite every effort being made to preserve anonymity it should be made clear to informants that such anonymity may be compromised unintentionally.

(*Principles of Professional Responsibility*, 1971, para. 1,c)

Protecting privacy extends far beyond changing names, places, and other identifying features in a final report. These are minimal requirements of anonymity. However, every ethnographer must realize that fieldnotes can become public knowledge if subpoenaed by a court. In doing research on illicit drug use, one student made lengthy interviews with local drug dealers and observed their purchase of illicit drugs. One day she discovered that her primary informant's "contact" in the illicit marketing system had been arrested, placing her informant in immediate jeopardy. When it became apparent that her fieldnotes and transcribed interviews might become of interest to law enforcement officials, she immediately eliminated all names and initials from the notes. Even so, it probably would have been impossible to protect the identity of her informant unless she had taken the further step of destroying the notes, an act that may well have been an illegal destruction of evidence. In another instance, an ethnographer studying a local school system collected data about a teachers' strike. After a suit between the union and the school board developed, the possibility arose that his fieldnotes would be subpoenaed by the court. Although neither of these cases materialized, each threat placed the ethnographers in an ethical dilemma. One must continually ask, "How can I maintain the anonymity of my informants?" A serious consideration of this ethical principle might, in some cases, lead to the selection of an alternate research project. At a minimum it should mean use of pseudonyms in both fieldnotes and final reports.

Don't Exploit Informants

There should be no exploitation of individual informants for personal gain. Fair return should be given them for all services.
(*Principles of Professional Responsibility,* 1971, para. 1,d)

Personal gain becomes exploitative when the informant gains nothing or actually suffers harm from the research. Every ethnographer bears a responsibility to weigh carefully what might constitute a "fair return" to informants. When conducting lengthy interviews, one might consider payment of an hourly wage, although such an offer would insult some informants. Sometimes an informant will gain directly from the results of the investigation; this possibility increases to the extent that informants have some say in the aims of the research. An ethnography often describes some part of an informant's culture in a way that gives the informant new insight and understanding. A copy of the ethnographic description might be fair return, but there are also less direct ways in which a project can have value to an informant. Students who study the culture of the elderly inevitably find that their informants relish the opportunity to reminisce about the past and talk to a younger, interested listener. An obvious value to many informants is the opportunity to assist a student in learning about another way of life. Even the simple gain of participating in a research project can be sufficient for many informants to talk to an ethnographer. Although "fair return" will vary from one informant to the next, the needs of informants for some gain from the project must not be ignored.

Make Reports Available to Informants

In accordance with the Association's general position on clandestine and secret research, no reports should be provided to sponsors that are not also available to the general public and, where practicable, to the population studied.

(Principles of Professional Responsibility, 1971, para. 1,g)

When students in my classes follow the steps in this book to do ethnography, I encourage them to make their papers available to their informants. If they study a public situation anonymously, this becomes unnecessary. For informants who would not understand the report, as in the case of a first-grade class, an oral presentation may be in order. This principle does not mean we should insist that informants read our reports; it does mean that what is written for teachers, colleagues, or the general public should also be available to informants.

This brief list of ethical principles does not exhaust the issues that will arise when doing research. The ethnographer has important responsibilities to the public and to the scholarly community. The full statement of *Principles of Professional Responsibility* adopted by the Council of the American Anthropological Association offers a rich source of additional principles for guiding our decision making. Every ethnographer should study this document as well as those developed by other associations involved in social science research.

Chapter Three

THE ETHNOGRAPHIC RESEARCH CYCLE

The ethnographer has much in common with the explorer trying to map a wilderness area. The explorer begins with a general problem, to identify the major features of the terrain; the ethnographer wants to describe the cultural terrain. Then the explorer begins gathering information, going first in one direction, then perhaps retracing that route, then starting out in a new direction. On discovering a lake in the middle of a large wooded area, the explorer might walk around it, then walk over familiar territory to measure the distance of the lake from the edge of the woods. The explorer would take frequent compass readings, check the angle of the sun, take notes about prominent landmarks, and use feedback from each observation to modify earlier information. After weeks of investigation, the explorer would probably find it difficult to answer the question, "What did you find?" Like an ethnographer, the explorer is seeking to describe a wilderness area rather than trying to "find" something.

Most social science research has more in common with the petroleum engineer who already has some detailed maps of the same wilderness area. The engineer has a specific goal in mind: to find oil or gas buried far below the surface. Before the engineer even begins an investigation, a careful study will be made of the maps which show geological features of the area. Then, knowing ahead of time the kinds of features that suggest oil or gas beneath the surface, the engineer will go out to "find" something quite specific. A great deal of social science research begins with a similar clear idea of something to find; investigators usually know what they are looking for.

In actual research practice this difference can be expressed in two research patterns. While other social science investigators tend to follow a *linear* pattern of investigation, the ethnographer tends to follow a *cyclical* pattern. Let's look briefly at an example of the linear sequence in social science research, after which we shall discuss the cyclical pattern ethnographers use.

McCord and McCord (1958), in their study of criminality, followed a typical linear sequence (Figure 3). They set out to see if parental role models influenced sons to engage in criminal behavior or to avoid such behavior. It isn't necessary to consider all the details of their study to see how they followed a linear sequence of activities outlined below.

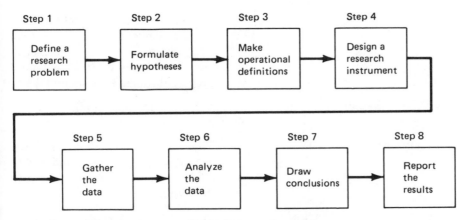

FIGURE 3. Linear Sequence in Social Science Research

STEP ONE: Define a research problem.

The McCords began by defining the research problem as the relationship between family environment and the causation of crime.

STEP TWO: Formulate hypotheses.

The study formulated numerous hypotheses about the relationship between parental attitudes, behavior, and discipline on the criminal activity (or absence of such activity) of sons. For example, they hypothesized that if fathers were deviant (criminals, promiscuous, etc.), their deviance would be reflected in criminality among sons, and "sons would imitate their deviant fathers, if the fathers are affectionate toward them."

STEP THREE: Make operational definitions.

The study defined words and phrases like "deviance" and "parental role model" in specific terms that would enable researchers to agree when they had identified deviant behavior.

STEP FOUR: Design a research instrument.

The study used previously collected data from interviews and observations. The main research instrument at the time of the study

27

was a set of rating instructions used by independent raters who read over this earlier data. The instrument could not be designed until Steps 1 through 3 had been taken.

STEP FIVE: Gather the data.

This was done using a group of independent raters.

STEP SIX: Analyze the data.

The data were then matched against the hypotheses and examined for new findings unrelated to the hypotheses.

STEP SEVEN: Draw conclusions.

Many conclusions arose from the study, including, for example, the one that paternal deviance was reflected in criminal behavior among sons.

STEP EIGHT: Report the results.

When the analysis had been completed, and conclusions drawn, the McCords then wrote up the results for publication.

In actual practice, the linear sequence outlined above is sometimes modified by the investigator. For example, one person may not formulate hypotheses (thus excluding Step Two), preferring to generate testable hypotheses as a conclusion to the study. But the general sequence remains. A research problem is defined before data can be collected; data analysis proceeds only after data is collected; the problem or the research instrument do not change midway through the project; and writing the final report does not lead to new questions and the collection of more data to be included in that report.

I believe ethnography seldom fits this linear model; instead, the major tasks follow a kind of cyclical pattern, repeated over and over again, which is outlined in Figure 4. In the remainder of this chapter I want to discuss each of the major activities in this cycle; in doing so I will give an overview of the twelve D.R.S. steps that make up Part Two of this book.

SELECTING AN ETHNOGRAPHIC PROJECT

The cycle begins with the selection of a research project. Perhaps the first thing ethnographers must consider is the *scope* of their investigation. Wolcott (1967) selected a Kwakiutl village in British Columbia with a population

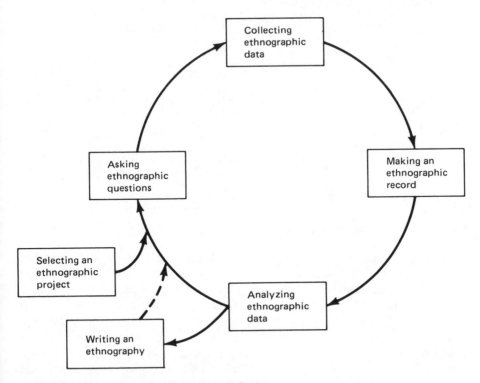

FIGURE 4. The Ethnographic Research Cycle

of about 125 people. Hicks' study of Little Laurel Valley (1976) focused on ten different settlements with a total population of about 1300 people. With a colleague I did ethnographic research on a small urban bar (Spradley and Mann 1975). Oscar Lewis spent a number of years studying a single family (1963). The scope of research can range along a continuum from *macro-ethnography* to *micro-ethnography*. Figure 5 shows this continuum and some of the social units that ethnographers have studied.

Let's begin at the macro- end of the continuum. Some ethnographers have attempted to describe the culture of a complex society consisting of numerous communities and with national institutions. Jules Henry, for example, studied American culture. In his classic book *Culture Against Man* (1963) he begins with the following statement: "This book is about contemporary American culture—its economic structure and values, and the relation of these to national character, parent-child relations, teenage problems and concerns, the schools, and to emotional breakdown, old age, and war. This is not an objective description of America, but rather a passionate ethnography" (1963:3). Moving down the continuum, Boas, in his research on the Kwakiutl, studied multiple communities (1966). Single-community studies represent the most abundant type of ethnographic research in an-

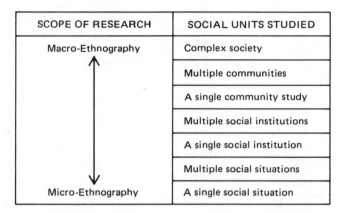

SCOPE OF RESEARCH	SOCIAL UNITS STUDIED
Macro-Ethnography	Complex society
	Multiple communities
	A single community study
	Multiple social institutions
	A single social institution
	Multiple social situations
Micro-Ethnography	A single social situation

FIGURE 5. Variations in Research Scope

thropology, ranging over the map from villages in India to a single band of Bushmen on the Kalahari Desert. Other ethnographers have focused on several social institutions within a single community. For example, Rohlen (1974) studied a Japanese white-collar organization, a modern bank, and his ethnography included information on closely related institutions such as the employees' union and employees' families. One can narrow the scope of ethnography still further to study a single social institution such as friendship, as Jacobson did among elites in urban Uganda (1973), or a flea market as Maisel did in California (1974). Within a single social institution, it is entirely possible to narrow the scope of research even further and focus on several related social situations. For example, our ethnography of Brady's Bar (Spradley and Mann 1975) focused only on those social situations important to the cocktail waitresses. We wanted to describe the world of the bar from their perspective to better understand the role of women in that bar. Finally, at the micro-ethnography end of the continuum, one may study a single social situation. Irvine (1974), for example, selected a single type of social situation, the *greetings* that occur between Wolof individuals. In our own society, classrooms, street corners, busses, and restaurants offer numerous social situations that can be studied ethnographically.

Macro-ethnography requires many years of research and often involves numerous ethnographers. On the other hand, micro-ethnography of a single social situation can be done in a much shorter time. For this reason, in this book I will stress doing micro-ethnography. However, the techniques of data collection and analysis are identical to those used in doing a project of much larger scope. It is possible to follow the D.R.S. Method as developed in this book for studying a single, isolated social situation, or for doing ethnography of much larger scope.

I have suggested that ethnography is usually done with a single general problem in mind: to discover the cultural knowledge people are using to organize their behavior and interpret their experience. Such a general goal encourages the ethnographer to study whatever informants feel is important in a particular cultural scene. However, many ethnographers select their research projects on the basis of a more limited problem. Hymes has identified three modes of ethnographic inquiry which can help us delineate the focus of a project (1978). *Comprehensive* ethnography seeks to document a total way of life. The ethnographer doing comprehensive ethnography in a village would, through participant observation, try to describe a wide range of customs, hoping to cover most areas of the community before completing the research. *Topic-oriented* ethnography narrows the focus to one or more aspects of life known to exist in the community. For example, an ethnographer might select a topic such as kinship, drinking behavior, or adoption. As one's ethnographic knowledge of a culture increases, it becomes possible to engage in what Hymes calls *hypothesis-oriented* ethnography. Hypotheses about the influence of child-rearing practices on adult personality have oriented numerous ethnographic projects in anthropology (Whiting, Child, and Lambert 1966). The research still follows the cycle outlined in Figure 4, but the initial selection of a project and data collected are influenced by a set of hypotheses.

In Step One, "Locating a Social Situation," we will return to the task of selecting an ethnographic research project; there I will identify six primary criteria that can be used for locating a setting in which to do a micro-ethnography project.

ASKING ETHNOGRAPHIC QUESTIONS

Ethnographic fieldwork begins when you start asking ethnographic questions. That seems evident enough when conducting interviews, but even the simplest observations and fieldnote entries involve asking questions. Assume for a moment that you begin riding a city bus as an ethnographer. The bus stops at a busy intersection and you watch as people board the bus, the doors close, and the driver pulls out into the intersection. You wait until everyone has taken a seat, then record the following statement in your fieldnotes: "Three people got on the bus at the Snelling Avenue bus stop, a woman and two boys. They each went to three separate empty seats and all selected a place next to the window." You have answered several implicit questions, questions you asked without realizing it:

1. Who got on the bus?
2. What were the sex and age of the new passengers?
3. What did they do after boarding the bus?
4. Where did each sit?

Instead of these questions, you could have asked such things as, "How tall is each new passenger?" "What is each passenger wearing?" and "Where does each one look as they move down the aisle?" These questions would have led to different entries in your fieldnotes.

In most forms of social science research, the questions asked by the researcher tend to come from *outside* the cultural scene. Investigators from one cultural scene (professional social science) draw on their frame of reference to formulate questions. They then will go to another cultural scene to interview or make observations. Without realizing it they tend to assume that questions and answers are separate elements in human thinking. In the study of other cultures this assumption usually leads to distortions.

Ethnography begins with a different assumption: that the question-answer sequence is a single element in human thinking. Questions always imply answers. Statements of any kind always imply questions. This is true even when the questions or answers remain unstated. In doing participant observation for ethnographic purposes, as far as possible, *both questions and answers must be discovered in the social situation being studied*. Black and Metzger have summarized this point of view:

It is basic to communications theory that you don't start getting any information from an utterance or event until you know what it is in response to—you must know what question is being answered. It could be said of ethnography that until you know the question that someone in the culture is responding to you can't know many things about the responses. Yet the ethnographer is greeted, in the field, with an array of *responses*. He needs to know what question people are *answering* in their every act. He needs to know which questions are being taken for granted because they are what "everybody knows" without thinking. . . . Thus the task of the ethnographer is to discover questions that seek the relationships among entities that are conceptually meaningful to the people under investigation (1964:144).

A major feature of the D.R.S. Method as it is developed in the following chapters will be to show you how to discover questions in the social situation you study. As you go through the ethnographic research cycle you will discover new questions to ask; these will guide your data collection. Then, when you analyze your data, new ethnographic questions will come to light, leading you to repeat the cycle. This process will continue throughout your investigation.

There are three major kinds of ethnographic questions, each leading to different kinds of observations in the field. All ethnography begins with broad *descriptive questions* (Step Four) such as "What people are here?" "What are they doing?" and "What is the physical setting of this social situation?" Later, after using these kinds of questions to guide your observations, and after analyzing your initial data, you will move on to discovering both *structural questions* (Step Six) and *contrast questions* (Step Seven).

These will guide you to make more focused observations. For now it is enough to remember that all participant observation involves the discovery and use of ethnographic questions to guide what you see and hear.

COLLECTING ETHNOGRAPHIC DATA

The second major task in the ethnographic research cycle (Figure 4) is collecting ethnographic data. By means of participant observation, you will observe the activities of people, the physical characteristics of the social situation, and what it feels like to be part of the scene. During the course of fieldwork, whether one studies a tribal village for a year or airline stewardesses for a few months, the types of observation will change. You will begin by making broad *descriptive* observations, trying to get an overview of the social situation and what goes on there (Step Four). Then, after recording and analyzing your initial data, you will narrow your research and begin to make *focused* observations (Step Seven). Finally, after more analysis and repeated observations in the field, you will be able to narrow your investigation still further to make *selective* observations (Step Ten). However, even as your observations become more focused, you will continue making general descriptive observations until the end of your field study. These three types of observation correspond to the three types of ethnographic questions. The progression from one type of observation to another is shown in Figure 6.

MAKING AN ETHNOGRAPHIC RECORD

The next step in the research cycle, following fast on the heels of each observation period, is making an ethnographic record. This includes taking fieldnotes, taking photographs, making maps, and using any other means to record your observations. This ethnographic record builds a bridge between observation and analysis. Indeed, most of your analysis will rely heavily on what you have recorded. In Step Three I will discuss strategies for making an ethnographic record.

ANALYZING ETHNOGRAPHIC DATA

The next step in the cycle cannot wait until you have collected a large amount of data. In ethnographic inquiry, analysis is a process of question-discovery. Instead of coming into the field with specific questions, the ethnographer analyzes the field data compiled from participant observation to discover questions. You need to analyze your fieldnotes after each period

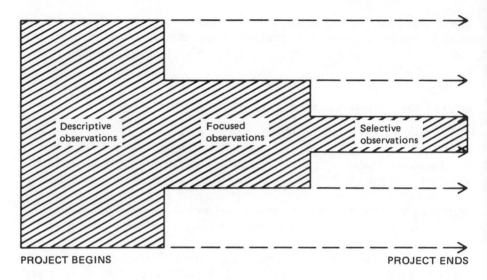

Participant observation begins with wide-focused *descriptive observations*. Although these continue until the end of the field project, as indicated by the broken lines, the emphasis shifts first to *focused observations* and later to *selective observations*.

FIGURE 6. Changes in the Scope of Observation

of fieldwork in order to know what to look for during your next period of participant observation. In this book we will examine four major kinds of ethnographic analysis: *domain* analysis (Step Six), *taxonomic* analysis (Step Eight), *componential* analysis (Step Ten), and *theme* analysis (Step Eleven). An experienced ethnographer may conduct these different forms of analysis simultaneously throughout the research period. The beginner can do them in sequence, learning to do each in turn before moving on to the next. Participant observation and recording fieldnotes, then, are always followed by data analysis, which leads to finding new ethnographic questions, more data collection, more fieldnotes, and more analysis. And so the cycle continues until your project nears completion.

WRITING AN ETHNOGRAPHY

This last major task in the research cycle occurs toward the end of a research project. However, it can also lead to new questions and more observations. Writing an ethnography forces the investigator into a new and more intensive kind of analysis. Those who begin their writing early and when they still can make observations will find that writing becomes part of the research cycle.

Ethnographic research involves an open-ended inquiry; it requires constant feedback to give the study direction. Ethnographers can only plan ahead of time the course of their investigation in the most general sense. Each of the major tasks in the research cycle act as a compass to keep you on track. If you confuse ethnography with the more typical linear pattern of research in the social sciences, you will confront unnecessary problems. Those who think of ethnography as a linear sequence tend to collect fieldnotes week after week and soon become overwhelmed with a mass of unorganized data. They have difficulty knowing when they have enough information on any topic. An even greater problem arises when they wait until all the data is in before beginning intensive analysis. New questions arise from the data; one cannot ask these questions because it is difficult or impossible to return to the field. Gaps in the information appear with no way to fill in the missing data.

Awareness of the ethnographic research cycle can keep you from losing your way in even the smallest project. Doing participant observation quickly immerses the ethnographer in a large amount of primary data. It is not uncommon for undergraduates who conduct research for only a few hours a week to compile ten to fifteen pages of fieldnotes each week. Ethnographers who spend several hours each day doing participant observation will have proportionately larger amounts of field data. Every now and then, during a field project, you need to climb a very tall tree and gain a broad perspective on how far you have come, what tasks lie ahead, and which direction you should take. By understanding that all ethnography goes through a fundamental cycle, you keep from losing sight of the forest because of the trees.

Part Two

THE DEVELOPMENTAL RESEARCH SEQUENCE

Part Two is based on an important assumption, one that has influenced the design of the remainder of this book: *the best way to learn to do ethnography is by doing it.* Each step contains the following elements:

Objectives: A brief statement of the learning goals at each particular stage in the ethnographic process.

Concepts: A discussion of the basic concepts necessary to achieving the learning goals at each particular stage.

Tasks: A specific set of tasks, which when completed enable one to achieve the objectives.

It is no accident that the title of each step is an activity—"Locating a Social Situation," "Doing Participant Observation," "Making an Ethnographic Record," and so on. These activities, steps in the larger Developmental Research Process, lead to an original ethnographic description.

I cannot emphasize too strongly that each successive step depends on reading the preceding step and *doing the tasks* identified in that step. If you read the remainder of this book in the same way as the first part, it will tend to result in a distorted understanding of participant observation. In short, each step in Part Two is designed to be *done* as well as *read.*

Finally, I want to remind the reader that Part Two focuses exclusively on doing participant observation. This focus will enable the reader to acquire a higher degree of mastery than is possible when using multiple research techniques. Depending on available time and background, one can easily combine the tasks that follow with ethnographic interviewing and observing in more than one social situation.

It is well to keep in mind from the beginning of a research project that the end result will be a written cultural description, *an ethnography.* An ethnographer may describe only a small segment of the culture in a brief article or paper for a course in ethnographic research. On the other hand, the ethnographer may end up writing a book or several books to describe the culture. In Step Twelve, I discuss some strategies for writing an ethnography. One of the most important ones is to *begin writing early.* If the ethnographer waits until after all the data are collected to begin writing, it will be too late to follow the leads that writing creates. Another reason to begin writing early is to simplify the task. Most people contemplate the task of writing a thirty-page report as formidable; writing ten three-page reports seems much less difficult.

In order to facilitate the writing task and make it part of the research process, I have made a list of brief topics, listed separately in Appendix B at the end of the book, that an ethnographer can write about while conducting research. Each writing task is designed to fit in with the particular stage of research. I envision a few pages written in rough draft form. Then, when you sit down to write the final ethnography, the task will be simplified as you revise these brief papers. It may be useful to read Step Twelve and review the writing tasks in Appendix B before starting the D.R.S. steps.

OBJECTIVES
1. To understand the role of social situations in beginning participant observation.
2. To identify the criteria for selecting the best social situation for participant observation.
3. To locate several possible social situations for doing ethnographic research.

Ethnographers have done participant observation in such a variety of settings that there appears to be little in common among research sites. From a remote tribal village in India (McCurdy 1971) to an Eskimo hunting group in northern Alaska (Nelson 1969), from a self-service restaurant in Helsinki, Finland (Kruse 1975), to a bus in Tulsa, Oklahoma (Nash 1975), ethnographers have conducted participant observation. Their search for the cultures people use to order their lives has taken them to fishing boats and city zoos, tribal hunting bands and high-rise apartment complexes, airport waiting rooms and large mental hospitals, nomadic tribes of the Sahara Desert and street corners in Washington D.C.

This enormous diversity of research sites can obscure an important common feature in all settings. Wherever the ethnographer may go and whatever the size of the social unit (a street corner, a village, a town, a city), all participant observation takes place in *social situations*. The first step in doing ethnography by means of participant observation is to locate a social situation. By understanding this concept and its role in the research project, you can easily find interesting and workable places for conducting your research. In this step we will examine the nature of social situations and several important criteria for making the best initial selection.

SOCIAL SITUATIONS

Every social situation can be identified by three primary elements: *a place, actors,* and *activities.* In doing participant observation you will locate yourself in some place; you will watch actors of one sort or another and become involved with them; you will observe and participate in activities. These primary elements do not exhaust the social and cultural meaning of social situations, but they do serve as a springboard into understanding them. Most important, by focusing on a single social situation you will greatly simplify the task of beginning your ethnographic research. It will help to think of social situations in terms of the following figure:

Place

Any physical setting can become the basis for a social situation as long as it has people present and engaged in activities. A *street* where people cross, a *bank window* where people line up and transact business, an *ocean pier* where people loiter and fish, a *bus door* through which people enter and exit the bus, and a *grocery-store check-out counter* where groceries are rung up, paid for, and bagged are all social situations. Each of these places offers rich opportunities for participant observation.

The ethnographer begins with a single, identifiable place for participant observation. However, it is often useful to think of a social situation as a *kind of place*. For example, one beginning ethnographer began observing on a specific bus that ran along Grand Avenue in St. Paul, Minnesota. However, it soon became clear that she could not do all her research on that specific bus, so she treated all the "Grand Avenue busses" as a single kind of place. She could have enlarged this category to "city busses" and treated them all as a kind of place, a social situation with various actors and activities. When Nelson (1969:228-45) studied Eskimo hunting, he treated many different locations for hunting seals as a single kind of place: *breathing holes*. He did not do all his observing at a single breathing hole since this would have greatly limited his discoveries. As he observed at a variety of breathing holes, he saw Eskimo hunters engaged in a complex set of activities. Another distinct kind of place, "the ice edge," is the basis for another kind of seal hunting and another distinct social situation. In your research you may observe at a single, specific location or at a single, identifiable kind of place with several locations; in either case you will be doing participant observation in a physical place, which is a primary element of any social situation.

Actors

Every social situation includes people who are considered particular kinds of actors. A businessman, a widow, and a child line up at a supermarket check-out counter. All become *customers* (a kind of actor) for the brief period of time they are in this social situation. At a busy intersection people become street crossers; on a bus they become bus riders and a bus driver; at seal holes and at the edge of the sea ice they become hunters. In Brady's Bar, where my colleague and I did ethnographic research, the people became one or another kind of customer, employee, or manager (Spradley and Mann 1975). As you search for a social situation for doing participant observation, you will need to keep in mind this second basic element, the kinds of actors people become.

When we first enter a social situation it is often difficult to know what kind of actors are present. All the investigator sees are people; with repeated observations one begins to notice the differences in clothing, behavior, demeanor, terms of identity, and other features that people use to identify the various actors in the situation. For example, when Northrop (1978) began observing people running on an indoor track, they all appeared to be "people who were running." Later, several distinct types of actors emerged, including *newcomers, visitors, regulars, track team members,* and *long-distance runners.* In selecting a social situation it isn't necessary to distinguish various types of actors; one only needs to know that people are present who are actors because they are engaging in some kind of activity, even if it is merely loitering.

Activities

The third primary element in every social situation is the activities that take place. At first, the ethnographer may see only a stream of behavior, hundreds of acts that all seem distinct. With repeated observations individual acts begin to fall into recognizable patterns of activity like hunting, sprinting, ordering drinks, selecting a seat on the bus, and bagging groceries at the supermarket check-out counter.

Sometimes sets of activities are linked together into larger patterns called *events.* Taking inventory in a supermarket, holding a track meet at a college, taking a hunting trip, holding a revival meeting in a church, and graduating from high school are all events made up of many different activities. Actually, the line between an activity and an event is often difficult to clearly identify. When the ethnographer begins research it may be impossible to know whether different activities constitute an event. Events often occur in many different social situations: a wedding, for example, may involve *the rehearsal,* the *wedding breakfast,* the *marriage ceremony,* the *reception,* and the *chase.* As the actors involved in a wedding move from place to place

41

and do many different things, an ethnographer from another culture would not know these activities were all linked together into a larger event called a "wedding." It is best to begin participant observation by observing and recording activities (the smaller units of behavior) in a social situation; as work proceeds, the structure of events will become clear.

Related Social Situations

It is usually best to begin ethnography by locating a *single* social situation. However, you may decide to begin with several closely related social situations. Or, once your research is under way, you may want to expand it to include several. In either case it is useful to identify three main ways social situations can be related.

1. Clusters of Social Situations. Even the simplest social situation which you thought involved a single location may turn out to include a cluster of social situations. Let's say you decide to become a participant observer at a nearby playground that covers half a city block. You can observe all the actors and activities from a single observation post. On a brief visit it appears to be a social situation: you observe a group of children playing on the swings and climbing bars; their parents are helping them or sitting on a bench beside the play area. But on subsequent visits and with more observations you discover that you are really studying a cluster of closely related social situations that include (1) the swings, (2) the bench where parents sit, (3) the sidewalk that bisects the park and is used for walking and skating, and (4) the embankment at the far end where teenagers congregate to talk and smoke. A cluster of social situations, as in this example, is linked by physical proximity (see Figure 7). The four situations at the playground can all be observed from a single place; they are connected in space. At Brady's Bar, although it was a small establishment, we discovered a cluster of social situations including the main bar, the waitress stations, the tables, and the telephone (Spradley and Mann 1975).

Sometimes the places included in a cluster of social situations may appear quite arbitrary. For example, in observing at the playground you may also be able to see automobiles and bicycles on the street, a man mowing his lawn at a distant house, and two telephone linemen repairing wires about fifty yards south of the playground. Should all of these actors and activities be included in a related cluster of social situations? Eventually you will want to try and decide on the basis of what the people in the playground think are related. For purposes of research, and especially for getting started in participant observation, it is not necessary to solve this problem. You can select a single social situation, expand your observations to take in a few that appear related, and leave others until later or simply exclude them from your research if they prove to be unimportant to the people you are studying.

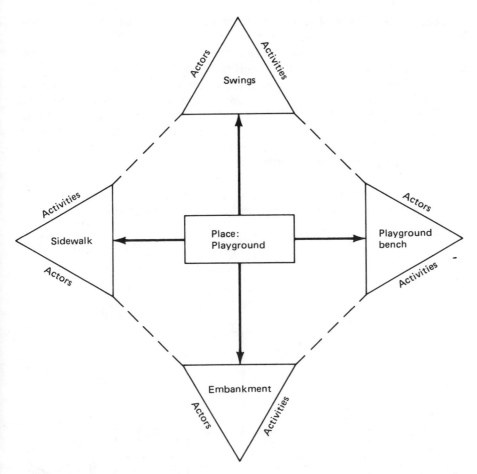

FIGURE 7.   A Cluster of Social Situations

2. A Network of Social Situations.   In addition to social situations linked together by physical proximity, others are connected because the same people are actors in different situations. In complex societies people move about from place to place, interacting with a wide range of other people. A student may participate in the following social situations in the course of a single morning: family breakfast, bus stop, chemistry laboratory, library study hall, and restaurant. Although these constitute a network of social situations for this particular student, the great variety of people make it difficult to do participant observation at all these places.

As ethnographers, we are interested in those networks of social situations where the *same group of people* share in the activities. Consider the following example. David Gordon set out to study a religious movement in Chicago called the "Jesus People" (1974). For a period of eight months he engaged in participant observation to discover the patterns of culture common to this group. He observed in one social situation they called "Bible studies," but the Jesus People were involved in a network of social situations, all of which eventually became sites for Gordon's research. These included Bible studies, revival meetings, street witnessing, marches, speaking engagements in churches and schools, and appearances on radio and television talk shows. This was not merely a single person moving through different situations, but an organized group of people who shared a *network of social situations*. We can represent a set of linked social situations that form a network by the diagram in Figure 8.

3. Social Situations with Similar Activities.   Social situations can become linked for the investigator in a third way: through the similarity in activities.

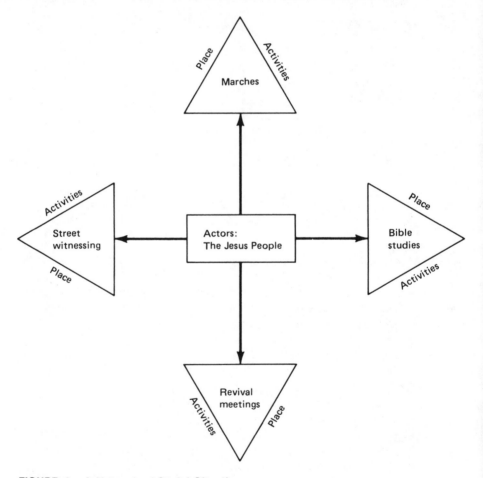

FIGURE 8. A Network of Social Situations

As your research progresses, you may want to expand it by identifying a single kind of activity (for example, swimming, waiting in line, buying used cars), then finding other places to observe similar activities. For instance, if you studied swimming, you could conduct observations in backyard swimming pools, rivers, lakes, and public pools, all the time focusing on this one kind of activity.

We can contrast activities in a single social situation with an activity in several social situations by looking briefly at two studies that focused on cultural rules for standing in line. Ferry (1978) selected a single social situation, the credit department of a large department store. He stationed himself at a convenient place where several lines would develop, with people seeking to cash checks or take care of other credit matters. Mann (1973), on the other hand, studied the same phenomenon but in many different places. He observed lines at theaters, football games, and other places where tickets were scarce. He also drew information from newspaper reports about long lines of people waiting for scarce tickets. Although the places and actors varied, his research focused on similar activities (see Figure 9).

To summarize: all social situations involve the three primary elements of place, actors, and activities. By keeping this in mind, the beginning ethnographer can easily locate one or more social situations for research. From the start you will probably see how your single social situation is linked to others. In time you may decide to include other social situations in your research project. Some will be related by physical proximity, forming a cluster of social situations. Others will be related by the same group of people who move from one place to another; then you may want to study a network of social situations. Finally, you may decide to focus on a single activity in a social situation and then extend your research by finding other places where similar activities occur.

SELECTION CRITERIA

Participant observation can serve many different purposes. Each investigator will have different reasons for selecting a particular setting for research. Wolcott (1967), for example, selected a Kwakiutl village and its school because of his interest in cross-cultural education. Walum (1974) selected a number of doors on a college campus where men and women entered buildings; she wanted to examine male and female interaction. The following criteria are designed with the beginning ethnographer in mind. If you follow these guidelines for selecting a research project, you will increase your chances for a successful study and also for learning the skills required for doing participant observation.

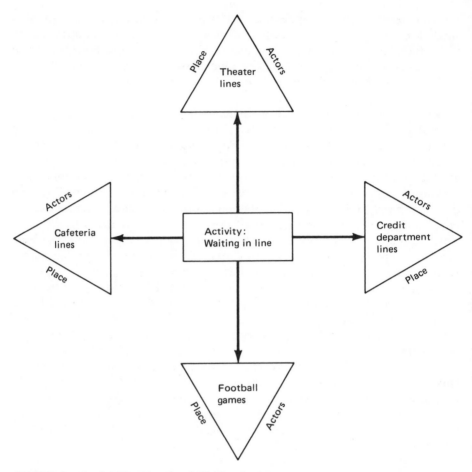

FIGURE 9. Social Situations and Similar Activities

Simplicity

I have already identified this criterion by suggesting that you select a *single* social situation. All participant observation is done in settings that fall somewhere along a continuum from the simplest social situation to the most complex clusters and networks of social situations. Consider the two projects identified in the previous paragraph: a Kwakiutl village and a set of doors on a college campus. Blackfish Village in British Columbia, where Wolcott did his participant observation, had a population of 125 children and adults, which represented only about thirteen families. However, his research took him to hundreds of different social situations—in the school, along village paths in the woods, in homes, on boats, along the waterfront, and in many other places. It took more than a year of intensive research to discover the culture of this tiny but complex native American village. Walum, on the other hand, studied a single type of social situation: doors through which people passed. Her study is no less sophisticated but only more limited in scope. Each study involved participant observation, but Wolcott's in a Kwakiutl village required a great deal more time, more involvement, and the use of many different strategies for collecting data.

The great advantage to the beginner of doing participant observation in simple settings is that one can *learn* to do ethnography in the course of actually doing *original research*. As you consider social situations that lie along the continuum from simple to complex, select one that lies closer to the simple end of the continuum. Later, with more experience, you will find it easier to navigate in more complex social settings.

Accessibility

Social situations offer varying degrees of accessibility. You can enter some settings easily, participate freely in the activities, and record your observations. Others offer easy access the first time and then become difficult or impossible to enter again. Consider several different social situations in a bank.

You could do participant observation at the entrance to a bank, at the lines in front of the tellers' windows, inside the employee restrooms, or inside the bank vault. Research at all these places would be interesting and useful in understanding the bank culture. However, there are striking differences in the degree of access to these social situations. The bank entrance offers the greatest accessibility for participant observation. If you studied the lines inside, you could easily enter, wait in line, cash a check, then leave. But repeated observations and participation would be more difficult. If you waited in line several times each day, sooner or later someone might become suspicious. Either at the entrance or in the lines you would probably want to inform the bank officials of your study and gain their permission. If you decided to observe in the employee restroom, even with permission your access would greatly decrease. And the bank vault could prove to be completely inaccessible. It would offer a unique challenge for research, but even with permission, much of your time would involve waiting to get into the vault and your activities would arouse considerable suspicion among the vault's users.

Consider some other social situations with varied degrees of access. Family dinners are less accessible than street corners. Corporation board meetings are less accessible than local playgrounds. Hospital operating rooms are less accessible than school lunchrooms. City jails are less accessible than city council meetings. All these settings offer significant opportunities for doing ethnography, but those that are less accessible present the beginning ethnographer with unnecessary complications for learning to do

47

research. If you select an operating room rather than a school lunchroom, for example, you will probably spend weeks learning valuable lessons about *gaining access*. However, you may have little chance to practice observing, recording, analyzing, and writing up your ethnographic data. As you consider your own interests and the remaining criteria, keep in mind that the greater the accessibility of a social situation, the better your opportunities for learning to do ethnography. Later, after having gained experience, you can undertake more challenging situations.

Unobtrusiveness

When anthropologists study in small, non-Western communities, they stand out like a giant sunflower in a field of daisies. Colin Turnbull, for example, a white anthropologist who towers well over six feet could not downplay his presence among African pygmies. He could not blend unnoticed into the crowd or participate in activities. One reason anthropological fieldwork requires many months of fulltime involvement is that the ethnographer must deal with all the responses to his or her presence. In doing participant observation for a short period, and with the goal of learning fieldwork skills, a low profile has distinct advantages.

Some settings offer much better possibilities for remaining unobtrusive than others. Public places like busses, restaurants, busy sidewalks, shopping malls, football games, airports, and libraries help to reduce the ethnographer's visibility. Hagstrom (1978) studied the process of becoming a regular at a small neighborhood restaurant. She remained unobtrusive by assuming the role of customer. She would enter the restaurant several mornings each week and sit in an out-of-the-way booth, where, almost unnoticed, she could drink coffee and write fieldnotes for more than an hour. Estenson (1978), on the other hand, could not remain so obscure in her study of picketers at an abortion clinic. At first she tried to observe from across a wide, busy street but could not see the details of behavior. When she moved closer, the picketers noticed her watching them and wondered whether she was ''one of them.'' Finally, to reduce her visibility, she moved inside the clinic itself and made her observations through a large window. Although she was able to conduct the research in an effective manner, many of the difficulties arose from her high visibility.

Participant observation almost always means some degree of unobtrusiveness. You may even seek the challenge that comes with a social situation where you will be highly visible. Rather than seeking to eliminate all obtrusiveness and concealing your presence completely, it is probably best to weigh carefully the extent to which a social situation will call attention to your activities. As a beginning ethnographer, you will increase the chances for successful research by selecting a setting that does not call direct attention to your activities.

Permissibleness

In every society some social situations cannot be studied without permission from someone. Deciding whether to seek permission, locating the persons who can grant permission, explaining the nature of your research, and finally gaining permission can become time-consuming activities. If the beginning ethnographer can circumvent some of these difficulties, it will facilitate both the research process and the learning of participant observation skills. We can consider three types of social situations from the perspective of acquiring permission for research.

In *free-entry* social situations, the ethnographer can do research without seeking permission. Edgerton (1978), for example, did ethnographic research on a large ocean beach in Southern California. Thousands of people congregated on this beach each day during the summer and he simply became an anonymous participant and observed what happened. Although he obtained permission for individual interviews, much of his data was gathered by participant observation. He observed, for example, the way people claimed a small territory for personal use, spread out their beach towels, and protected their belongings. It would have been virtually impossible to gain permission from all the people he watched. Nash (1975) did not need permission to ride the city bus in Tulsa, Oklahoma. Furthermore, it would have been impossible and unnecessary to ask all riders for permission to make observations. Many, if not all, public places offer free entry. In selecting a social situation for learning to do participant observation, those that offer free entry will help pave the way to a successful research project.

Limited-entry social situations require permission from one or more persons before conducting research. Private offices, barber shops, an alcoholism treatment center, hospital emergency room, and a private home represent limited-entry situations. Even public places like a school will usually require the permission of at least the principal and the teacher in whose classroom you make observations. In some schools you may even need to get the permission of each child's parents. Limited-entry social situations can become excellent places to do your first field study, provided the permission-gaining process goes smoothly. Verin (1978), for example, studied a classroom where deaf children were "mainstreamed" with hearing children. She approached the school principal and a teacher in one class; permission came easily and quickly. During her research she had the support and interest of the teacher; she sat in the back of the room and recorded what took place. Rather than eliminating limited-entry social situations from your list of possibilities, try to estimate the time and work involved in gaining permission. A phone call to the right person can help you decide whether you can gain permission easily or whether it will involve numerous delays. Seeking permission, if it doesn't become complicated and time consuming, can enrich the fieldwork learning experience.

Restricted-entry social situations, the third type, have a high probability that permission will be extremely difficult or impossible to acquire. Groups engaged in criminal activities, street gangs, secret societies, and closed meetings in churches or corporations all have restrictions that make participant observation difficult. If you had many months to gain the trust and confidence of members, you still might study any of these groups. Soloway and Walters (1977), for example, studied active heroin addicts, and Keiser (1969) did participant observation among the Vice Lords, a street gang. However, the difficulties in such situations mean that gaining permission can take weeks and even months of patient work. Once you have made a list of interesting social situations to study, it is best for the beginning fieldworker to cross off those that will present restricted entry problems.

Frequently Recurring Activities

In order to discover the cultural rules for behavior, you will need to observe a large sample of similar activities repeated over and over. If you select an isolated suburban intersection in order to study the cultural rules for crossing streets, you will observe far fewer instances of this activity than at a busy intersection downtown. An important criterion, then, for selecting a social situation is the *frequency of recurrent activities*. Ehrman (1978) studied *waiting behavior* at a busy airport and easily found hundreds of people waiting for an airplane departure. Had she decided instead to study *sleeping behavior* in public, an activity that did occur in the airport, the relative infrequency of sleeping would have limited her research. The goal is to select a social situation in which some activities frequently recur.

The frequency with which the same activities are repeated depends, in part, on the time selected for observation. If you go to a local supermarket to observe the check-out counters at 9:15 each morning, you may discover little activity. However, if you go during the peak rush period between five and six each evening, you will see the same activities repeated again and again. Beginning ethnographers often make the mistake of searching for social situations with a great variety of activities. Unless some are recurrent and acted out repeatedly, the situation will not serve your research purposes adequately. Because it is often difficult to anticipate the activities you will observe in a social situation, you may have to apply this criterion after your research is under way. You cannot observe everything; in deciding what to focus on, try to select those activities that recur with a relatively high frequency. Tolzmann (1978) studied an urban arcade located between a number of stores in a large city. At first she wanted to observe the dangers people encountered in this impersonal, public place. However, it soon became evident that she could not actually observe many instances of dangerous threats; they simply did not occur often enough. So she shifted her focus to those activities intended to maximize safety and reduce intrusion of personal space. Immediately she found numerous instances of such activities. The steps in the D.R.S. Method, as I have emphasized earlier, have a dual goal: to learn to do ethnography while at the same time actually conducting original research. You will achieve this dual purpose more readily if you carefully select a social situation in which activities are frequently repeated.

Participation

Ethnographers do not merely make observations, they also participate. Participation allows you to experience activities directly, to get the feel of what events are like, and to record your own perceptions. At the same time, the ethnographer can hardly ever become a complete participant in a social situation. In Step Two we will examine different degrees and forms of participation; at this point in selecting a social situation, you should look for ones that offer the best opportunities for participation.

Consider the possibilities for participation in two contrasting social situations. First, if you studied the tacit rules for behavior in a library you could easily participate by looking for books, sitting at tables, checking out books, and returning books. This personal involvement would enable you to test observations about what other people did in the library and to explore the culture more fully than you could do by observation alone. On the other hand, if you studied the behavior of a surgical team in an operating room of a hospital, you would undoubtedly have to remain a spectator. Although you could gather important data, even as a spectator you would not know the feelings and perceptions of a participant. Ethnographers frequently encounter situations that hold little opportunity for participation; they must then depend on observation alone and ethnographic interviews (see Spradley 1979). For example, in tribal societies the ethnographer probably won't get married, give birth to children, or go through a puberty rite, but will observe such events. In these cases, collecting data always depends on extensive ethnographic interviews.

As you consider possible social situations for research, try to imagine *how* you would participate. In the Seattle criminal court where I studied arraignment and sentencing of skid row men, I participated as a *spectator,* an accepted role in that court. In our research on cocktail waitresses, Mann (1976) became a full participant, taking employment as a cocktail waitress at Brady's Bar. Maisel (1974) studied a flea market where people bought and sold used goods. He participated by buying, browsing, and selling. Hayano (1978) studied the culture of a large urban poker parlor; he became a participant by playing poker. Singwi (1976) studied the cultural rules in a small restaurant through the role of waitress, while Hagstrom (1978) did a similar study but participated in the role of customer. The best social situations for learning to do ethnography offer ample opportunity to partici-

51

pate in a natural way, and also allow you on occasion to act as an observer only, taking notes and watching others' activities. Kruft found this balance in studying a blood bank (1978). As a participant she went frequently to give plasma, to find out what one experiences as a blood donor. On most occasions it was necessary for her to wait her turn to give blood, during which time she was able to observe and take fieldnotes.

I have identified five criteria to be used in selecting a social situation for doing participant observation: (1) simplicity, (2) accessibility, (3) unobtrusiveness, (4) permissibleness, and (5) frequently recurring activities. Although these criteria cannot all be met to the highest degree in a single social situation, they are offered here as guidelines for making an initial choice. You will want to balance them against personal interest, time constraints, and theoretical concerns. As your skills at doing participant observation improve, some of the criteria will become less important. But the beginning ethnographer will acquire ethnographic skills more easily if fieldwork is done in a social situation selected on the basis of the five criteria.

Tasks

1.1 Make a list of at least fifty social situations in which one could engage in participant observation.

1.2 Identify the five or six best situations in terms of your own interests and the five selection criteria discussed.

OBJECTIVES
1. To become familiar with the role of participant observer.
2. To understand the different types of participation possible in ethnographic research.
3. To undertake a practice field observation.

Doing participant observation has many things in common with what everyone does in newly encountered social situations. I recall the day I was inducted into the United States Army. I reported to the induction center feeling like a stranger among all the other draftees and military personnel. As I took the oath of allegiance, underwent a physical exam, listened to orientation lectures, and left for Fort Ord, California, I frequently felt at a loss as to how to conduct myself. Because I could not participate with the ease of someone who had done prior service, I adapted by watching carefully what other people said and did. During the early weeks of basic training I continued to act much like a participant observer, trying to learn how to behave as a private in the Army. When walking about Fort Ord, I would watch other people to see if they saluted passing cars or people who looked like officers. Taking my cue from them, I would imitate their actions. Slowly I learned the culture of Army life, felt less like a stranger, and became an ordinary participant who gave little thought to the social situations I encountered.

If you select an unfamiliar social situation you can build on this common experience. Because you feel like a stranger, because you don't know the tacit rules for behavior, you will fall naturally into the role of participant observer. In this step we want to examine the differences between the *ordinary participant* in a social situation and the role you will assume for research purposes, the *participant observer*.

ORDINARY PARTICIPANT VERSUS PARTICIPANT OBSERVER

All human beings act as ordinary participants in many social situations. Once we learn the cultural rules, they become tacit and we hardly think about what we are doing. Consider, for instance, the ordinary participant who has crossed busy intersections thousands of times. This person approaches the street without thinking about the cultural rules for crossing. Watching the traffic, slowing to step off the curb, staying within the white lines, and weaving skillfully among the crowd of people coming from the other side, the ordinary participant's thoughts may be a million miles away. A participant observer, on the other hand, studying this common social situation, would seem, to all outward appearances, like an ordinary participant. The unseen differences would mostly remain hidden inside the investigator's head. Let us consider six major differences between the ordinary participant and the participant observer, differences you will need to become aware of each time you visit the setting of your research.

Dual Purpose

The participant observer comes to a social situation with two purposes: (1) to engage in activities appropriate to the situation and (2) to observe the activities, people, and physical aspects of the situation. The ordinary participant comes to that same situation with only one purpose: to engage in the appropriate activities. In the process of carrying out these actions, this person does not normally want to watch and record everything else that occurs, describe all the actors present, or make note of the physical setting.

Let's consider a common social situation, that of purchasing a soft drink from a vending machine. At Macalester College, "Coke machines," as they are called, stand at convenient places in many of the buildings on campus. I have frequently stopped to purchase a soft drink; one can see other faculty, students, and staff buying from these machines most any day. As an ordinary participant, I approach a Coke machine with a single purpose: to purchase a soft drink. Like most people, I am not interested in what steps I go through to operate the machine. I know them so well I act without thinking, putting my money in the slot, pushing the proper button, and taking a can of Coke or Seven-Up from the dispenser tray. If I have to wait for someone else to finish using the machine, I don't watch what they are doing *in order to* understand more fully their actions. I know what they are doing; I may look at the way they have dressed, or try to remember their name if I have heard it before. I act with the limited goals of an ordinary participant in this social situation.

The participant observer does not take this single-minded approach. Monsey (1978) undertook an ethnographic study of the way people interact with machines, especially vending machines. As a participant observer she made frequent purchases from Coke machines. To all outward appearances, she did what others did, but she approached each vending machine with an additional purpose: to watch her own actions, the behavior of others, and everything she could see in this social situation. When she had to wait her turn, she focused on how people interacted with the machine, the steps they went through to make their purchases, their reactions when the machines did not make proper change. Like all participant observers she operated with two purposes in mind at the same time.

Explicit Awareness

The complexity of social life requires that the ordinary participant exclude much from conscious awareness. If you go into a bank and find yourself waiting in line, you will ignore most of what goes on around you. You will not watch how far apart *each* person in line stands from the others, though you may notice the person behind you who stands too close. You will not try to pay attention to how quickly each person moves, how they stand, how they handle their belongings, the color of the carpet, the paths taken to leave the bank, or the hundreds of other things going on around you. To be sure, you might notice what the person in front of you says to the teller or when one line moves more quickly than the others, but most of what goes on around you will remain outside your awareness.

If human beings actively tried to remember and catalog *all* the activities, *all* the objects, *all* the information they could perceive, and if they did this *all* the time, they would experience what some scholars have called *overload*. Overload "refers to a system's inability to process inputs from the environment because there are too many inputs for the system to cope with" (Milgram 1970:1461). We all adapt to the potential threat of overload by paying less attention to information we do not need or want. This blocking occurs so frequently and so continuously that we could hardly survive without it.

We have all had experiences like the following that make us aware of how much we block out in the ordinary course of activities. John walks down the hallway on his way to class. He stops and purchases a Coke from the machine, continues to the end of the hallway, and enters the classroom. A friend sees him with the Coke and infers that John probably purchased it from the Coke machine down the hall. "Is that machine still out of Tab?" the friend asks. "I didn't notice," says John. Someone nearby says, "Did you notice if the print shop was open across the hall?" Again, John pleads ignorance. He probably "saw" the sign indicating the machine was still out of Tab as well as the print-shop door which stood wide open. But, like most of us would have done, he excluded them from explicit awareness.

The participant observer, in contrast, seeks to become explicitly aware of things usually blocked out to avoid overload. Increasing your awareness does not come easily, for you must overcome years of *selective inattention,* tuning out, not seeing, and not hearing. Monsey (1978), in her research on vending machines and their customers, had to force herself to pay attention to information she normally excluded. How did people open their soft drinks? What kind of noises did the machine make? How many people were in the hallway? How did people respond to notes taped to the machine? How did they respond to lights that indicated "sold out," to the presence of other people waiting for them to finish making a purchase, and to the many other details of activity at the Coke machine itself? Participant observation requires the ethnographer to increase his or her awareness, to raise the level of attention, to tune in things usually tuned out.

Wide-Angle Lens

All human beings use their perceptual skills to gather information about social situations. We are all *observers,* even when acting as ordinary participants. But what we watch and listen for remains limited to our immediate purpose of accomplishing some activity. Not only does the participant observer have a heightened sense of awareness, but he or she must also approach social life with a wide-angle lens, taking in a much broader spectrum of information.

Let's go back to the Coke machine in the hallway. Every person who uses a Coke machine must make some observations. You have to find out if it will take nickels or dimes or quarters; you need to find the slot in which to insert coins. You will have to look the machine over to discover where it dispenses its contents. You will have to listen to hear when the cans or bottles drop out of the machine. You will need to see if someone else is at the machine, requiring you to wait your turn. Observations such as these are part of all human activities.

As a participant observer studying the tacit cultural rules for using and interacting with vending machines, you would make much broader observations. Monsey (1978) observed all the people in the hallway. Watching those who approached the vending machines, she observed how they approached them and how they left them. She wrote down seeming trivia about all the sounds the machines made which communicated information to users who took those sounds for granted. She wrote down what people said to the machines, and watched them hitting and kicking them when the machines didn't deliver. She tried to describe the atmosphere around vending machines. Many of the things she observed an ordinary participant would have considered "unnecessary trivia," but, for the participant observer, a wide observational focus leads to some of the most important data.

The Insider/Outsider Experience

The ordinary participant in a social situation usually experiences it in an immediate, subjective manner. We see some of what goes on around us; we experience our own movements; we move through a sequence of activities as subjects, as the ones engaging in the activities. In short, we are *insiders.* Our experience of participating in a social situation takes on meaning and coherence from the fact that we are *inside* the situation, part of it.

The participant observer, on the other hand, will experience being both insider and outsider simultaneously. Consider people playing poker. Ordinary participants are part of the game. As outsiders, they act as subjects. Hayano (1978) decided to become a participant observer in poker parlors in Gardena, California. On an average weekend, six poker parlors draw several thousand people; Hayano played many thousands of hours of poker, listened to people talk, and observed their strategies for managing the game. As in *insider* he shuffled cards, dealt hands, made bids, bluffed, and both won and lost hands. As an *insider* he felt some of the same emotions during the course of the game that the ordinary participants felt. At the same time he experienced being an *outsider*, one who viewed the game and himself as *objects*. He had the uncommon experience of being a poker player and simultaneously observing himself and others behaving as poker players. He was part of the scene, yet outside the scene.

Although not unique to ethnographers doing research, this experience is much more common to those who do participant observation. You probably won't have this simultaneous insider/outsider experience all the time. On some occasions you may suddenly realize you have been acting as a full participant, without observing as an outsider. At other times you will probably be able to find an observation post and become a more detached observer. Doing ethnographic fieldwork involves alternating between the insider and outsider experience, and having both simultaneously.

Introspection

Many people look within themselves to assess how they feel about particular experiences. In routine, ordinary activities, such as crossing the street or purchasing a Coke from a vending machine, we do not become very introspective. We usually carry out these activities with a minimum of reference to our inner states. However, when an unexpected event occurs, such as an auto accident or failing an exam, we engage in more introspection.

As a participant observer, you will need to increase your introspectiveness. In a real sense, you will learn to use yourself as a research instrument. For example, in our research on Brady's Bar (Spradley and Mann 1975), Mann spent many evenings working as a cocktail waitress, fully experiencing the entire range of things that other waitresses experienced. Then, after work, often during debriefing conversations, she would try to find out what these experiences felt like, how she did things, what it felt like to work as a cocktail waitress. This kind of introspection of ordinary activities contrasts sharply with the ordinary participant who has learned to take the experience for granted. Introspection may not seem "objective," but it is a tool all of us use to understand new situations and to gain skill at following cultural rules.

Introspection will greatly enrich the data an ethnographer gathers through participant observation.

Record Keeping

Finally, unlike most ordinary participants, the participant observer will keep a detailed record of both objective observations and subjective feelings. This record can sometimes be made on the spot; at other times you will record it later, when you have left the social situation. The ordinary participant almost never records the details of routine activities like crossing streets, making phone calls, visiting a museum, going to a flea market, running in a gymnasium, or eating in a restaurant. In the next step we will discuss the making of an ethnographic record.

The role of participant observer will vary from one social situation to another, and each investigator has to allow the way he or she works to evolve. But as your role develops, you will have to maintain a *dual purpose:* you will want to seek to participate and to watch yourself and others at the same time. Make yourself *explicitly aware* of things that others take for granted. It will be important to take mental pictures with a *wide-angle lens,* looking beyond your immediate focus of activity. You will experience the feeling of being both an *insider* and an *outsider* simultaneously. As you participate in routine activities, you will need to engage in *introspection* to more fully understand your experiences. And finally, you will need to *keep a record* of what you see and experience. These six features of the participant-observer role distinguish it from what you already know as an ordinary participant.

TYPES OF PARTICIPATION

Any survey of participant observers would reveal great differences in the style of their research. One important contrast is the degree of their involvement, both *with* people and *in* the activities they observe. We can explore this variation by examining five types of participation that range along a continuum of involvement as shown below.

DEGREE OF INVOLVEMENT	TYPE OF PARTICIPATION
High	Complete
	Active
	Moderate
Low	Passive
(No involvement)	Nonparticipation

Nonparticipation

Let's begin at the bottom of the scale with the observer who has no involvement with the people or activities studied. It is entirely possible to collect data by observation alone. Sometimes this kind of research may be undertaken by an extremely shy individual who would like to conduct ethnographic fieldwork but wants to avoid involvement. Sometimes a particular social situation does not allow for any participation, but still holds possibilities for research.

Consider the ethnographic study of television programs. Bean (1976) set out to study the cultural themes in contemporary soap operas. She viewed various programs and read *The Soap Opera Newsletter*. She was able to identify a number of cultural themes and concluded that "soap operas contain a coherent expression of the principles on which the American family is based" (1976:97). Watching television offers many other opportunities for the nonparticipant to make observations. For example, a slightly less "staged" type of program that offers ethnographic possibilities is the football game. By watching numerous televised games, an ethnographer could discover not only the explicit rules for the game but also the tacit rules for wearing uniforms, staging half-time performances, communicating nonverbally, demonstrating affection for other team members, and even how to behave as a sports newscaster. Children's cartoons, commercial advertisements, newscasts, and the entire range of programs offer other opportunities for ethnographic study without involvement.

Passive Participation

The ethnographer engaged in passive participation is present at the scene of action but does not participate or interact with other people to any great extent. About all you need to do is find an "observation post" from which to observe and record what goes on. If the passive participant occupies any role in the social situation, it will only be that of "bystander," "spectator," or "loiterer."

Participant observation in public places often begins with this kind of detachment. I spent many hours as a spectator in the Seattle Criminal Court observing drunks, court clerks, other spectators, and the judge. To begin with no one knew my identity or what I was doing. Later, I became more active and interviewed the judge, talked with clerks, and developed close relationships with many of the men who appeared in court on drunk charges (Spradley 1970).

One can infer a great deal about the cultural rules people follow from the vantage point of a passive participant. If you stood outside the window of a hospital nursery and watched the nurses and infants, you would notice patterns of cultural behavior—ways to hold infants, how long to allow crying, and patterns for changing and feeding them. In this setting you might be required to remain outside the nursery window, but in many situations one can soon move from passive participant to more involvement.

Consider another example of passive participation. In her study of formal ballet classes, Hall (1976) received permission to make observations in six ballet studios. She had taken lessons herself for sixteen years at an earlier period of her life but decided to observe for ethnographic purposes. She visited two advanced classes in each of the studios for three weeks, then settled on observing three classes at one studio for two months. She did not enter into the class activities but stayed on the sidelines observing and taking notes. From her earlier experience as an ordinary participant, she moved on to observe in this passive manner. Later she interviewed ten members of an advanced class to supplement her observations.

Moderate Participation

Moving up the scale of involvement we come to the style of research described earlier in this chapter. Moderate participation occurs when the ethnographer seeks to maintain a balance between being an insider and an outsider, between participation and observation. Sanders' study of pinball players (1973) is a good example of moderate participation. He entered the scene of a West Coast pool hall as a "loiterer" and "game watcher," two roles that he observed were acceptable in this setting. From the start he kept careful fieldnotes, recording them after returning from a field trip. In time he played the machines, even developing particular preferences as regular players did, but he never achieved the skill or status of a regular.

Active Participation

The active participant seeks to *do* what other people are doing, not merely to gain acceptance, but to more fully learn the cultural rules for behavior. Active participation begins with observations, but as knowledge of what others do grows, the ethnographer tries to learn the same behavior. Richard Nelson sought to be an active participant during his research among the Eskimo. He writes:

The primary method of data collection throughout this study is based on observation, but observation of a special nature. This is not "participant observation" in the sense that most anthropologists have used the term. It involves much more than living in a community and participating in its daily life only to the extent that one is always there to watch what is going on. This kind of observation without actually becoming involved as a part of the activity or interaction might be termed passive participation.

The present study utilizes a technique which I prefer to call "active" or "full" participation. This means that in order to document techniques of hunting and travel, the ethnographer attempts to learn and master them himself—to participate in them to the fullest possible extent.

When full participation is used to document a technique such as a method of hunting, the ethnographer must learn to do it himself with at least the minimum proficiency necessary for success. In a sense, then, he observes others and learns from them, but he learns by observing himself as well. (1969:394).

Although active participation is an extremely useful technique, not all social situations offer the same opportunity as does Eskimo seal hunting. The ethnographer studying open heart surgery in a hospital or the dancing of professional ballerinas may have difficulty carrying out the same activities as those done by the surgeon or the dancer. Most ethnographers can find some areas in their research where active participation is feasible and even limited use of this technique will contribute to greater understanding.

Complete Participation

The highest level of involvement for ethnographers probably comes when they study a situation in which they are already ordinary participants. Nash (1975) rode the bus each day to the University of Tulsa and decided to do an ethnography of busriders. He was a complete participant, had learned the rules for riding the bus, and simply began to make systematic observations during the course of this daily activity. In another ethnographic study, Nash (1977) made use of his complete involvement in long-distance running to do ethnography of bus riders. He was a complete participant, had learned the hospital came about because, shortly after finishing graduate work, he became a patient. Becker studied jazz musicians, and writes:

I gathered the material for this study by participant observation, by participating with musicians in the variety of situations that make up their work and leisure lives. At the same time I made the study I had played the piano professionally for several years and was active in musical circles in Chicago (1963:83-84).

The examples of ethnographers who have turned ordinary situations in which they are members into research settings could go on and on. Indeed, in an excellent article, "Varieties of Opportunistic Research," Riemer (1977) reviews numerous studies based on complete involvement by anthropologists and sociologists, including home towns, cab driving, bars, police departments, prisoner-of-war activities, a chiropractic clinic, race tracks, carnivals, and even the Coast Guard Academy. The beginning ethnographer may want to follow these examples and search for opportunities close at hand. I would offer one word of caution: the more you know about a situation as an ordinary participant, the more difficult it is to study it as an ethnographer. It is no accident that ethnography was born and developed in the study of non-Western cultures. The *less* familiar you are with a social situation, the *more* you are able to see the tacit cultural rules at work.

As you make a final selection of a social situation to study, keep in mind the possibilities for involvement. The techniques you will learn in the following steps will serve you well at any degree of involvement, from nonparticipation to complete participation. Using these techniques you can discover the cultural knowledge underlying professional wrestling matches on television or the cultural rules for behavior in a college classroom. And once you have learned the strategies for asking ethnographic questions, collecting ethnographic data, and recording and analyzing that data, you can use these skills to understand the culture of more complex social worlds.

Tasks

2.1 **Do participant observation for thirty minutes in any unfamiliar social situation.**

2.2 **Record some fieldnotes and identify all problems encountered in assuming the role of participant observer.**

2.3 **Make a reconnaissance trip to one or more social situations you are considering for your ethnographic research. Make a final selection for your project.**

OBJECTIVES

1. To understand the nature of an ethnographic record.
2. To set up a fieldwork notebook.
3. To conduct the first period of participant observation and make a record of the experience.

The next step in the Developmental Research Sequence is to learn how to compile a record of research. Even before participant observation begins, the ethnographer will have impressions, observations, and decisions to record. By now you have selected a social situation for investigation and made an initial reconnaissance trip to that situation. Recording how you made the selection as well as first impressions will prove of great value later. In this step we will examine the nature of an ethnographic record, the kind of information to record, and practical steps for making it most useful for analysis and writing.

THE ETHNOGRAPHIC RECORD AND LANGUAGE USE

An ethnographic record consists of fieldnotes, tape recordings, pictures, artifacts, and anything else that documents the social situation under study. As Frake has pointed out, "A description of a culture, an *ethnography,* is produced from an *ethnographic record* of the events of a society within a given period of time, the 'events of a society' including, of course, informants' responses to the ethnographer, his queries, tests, and apparatus" (1964b:111).

During my own study of skid row men (Spradley 1970), I began by doing participant observation in the Seattle Criminal Court. Several times each week I would drive to the Public Safety Building in the heart of the business district of Seattle. I took the elevator to the seventh floor, waited until court began at 9:00 A.M., entered the court, and took a seat as a spectator. I watched the proceedings for the next hour, sometimes staying to observe other cases after the last drunk had been returned to jail. Soon I became a familiar person in the audience and began to receive nods of recognition from clerks, the judge, and the alcoholic counselor.

Many different things went into the ethnographic record during this time. I copied off the name of the court and the names of the judges and room numbers from the large wall directory near the elevator on the first floor of the Public Safety Building. I drew a map of the courtroom, describing the physical layout as I saw it. I counted the number of visitors who came to watch the proceedings in court, trying to describe some of their main characteristics. Here is a short excerpt from my fieldnotes:

At 9:00 A.M. a group of from 20–30 men were marched into the court through a side door. There were 40–45 people in the audience. The men stood in a double row to the left front of the courtroom. Immediately in front of the men were three officials of the court, probably clerks. To the left of the men, in the front center of the courtroom, was the judge. Judge Noe was not on duty so the judge pro tem was Lieme Puai. Directly in front of the judge was another clerk and the bailiff. As the men entered the room, their names were called off in a loud, official voice by the clerk nearest the judge. Each man stood at semiattention. Many had their hands clasped behind them. They all came from the city jail. They were all dressed very poorly, many unshaven. The group was a mixture of Negro, Indian, Eskimo, Caucasian, and other races.

The judge charged the group. "You men have been charged with public drunkenness or begging, which is in violation with the ordinances of the City of Seattle. The possible penalty: $500 fine and/or 180 days in jail. You have the right to an attorney. You may plead guilty or not guilty. If you want a trial you must pay for your own attorney. If you wish continuance, please indicate. If you plead guilty you forfeit your right to appeal to the Supreme Court. Please return to the docket. When you are called in you will enter a plea of guilty or not guilty. If you wish to make a statement you may do so."

Each man in court came out. His name was read off and then the clerk who was reading the sentences indicated to the man again that he had been charged with public drunkenness and asked what he would plead. Nearly every man said only one word: "Guilty." In the second group that came out, time from the entry to the courtroom as individuals until sentence was passed involved the following number of seconds on eight of the men where a time was taken: 25, 12, 20, 14, 34, 10, 35, 18. There were several men assisting in getting the men into the courtroom rapidly. One of these, I assume, was a jail attendant.

During the next year I took fieldnotes in court, recorded my own reactions to the process, collected information from the court records, took pictures of men on skid row, and recorded casual conversations with drunks, police officers, judges, clerks, and alcoholism treatment counselors. I tape recorded numerous interviews. I collected newspaper clippings, police department reports, and bulletin board notices posted at the alcoholism treatment center. And always, I made notes about my experiences actually doing the research. This record became the basis for writing an ethnography of tramp culture (Spradley 1970).

The major part of any ethnographic record consists of *written fieldnotes*. And the moment you begin writing down what you see and hear, you automatically encode things in language. This may seem a rather straightforward matter, but the language used in fieldnotes has numerous long-range consequences for your research. When anthropologists do ethnographic research in non-Western societies, they encounter striking language differences. In studying a Highland New Guinea tribe, for example, the first task is to learn the native language. Fieldnotes soon become filled with native terms, and it is easy to distinguish the ethnographer's language in the fieldnotes from the language of the people being studied.

When doing ethnography in your own society, however, it is easy to overlook language differences and thereby lose important clues to cultural meaning. The central question faced by every ethnographer when taking fieldnotes is *what language shall be used in making an ethnographic record?*

Consider, for a moment, the language variations that became part of my ethnographic record studying tramps:

1. *The investigator's native language.* Many of my fieldnotes were written in the ordinary language I use in everyday situations. Obviously, this included meanings drawn from as far back as my childhood.

2. *The language of social science.* Other entries in my fieldnotes came from the more abstract language of social science that I have learned as a professional anthropologist.

3. *The language of tramps.* I recorded what tramps said in court during informal conversations at the treatment center and also during interviews.

4. *Courtroom languages.* A specialized way of talking was used by the city attorney, court clerks, and the judge who presided over the daily arraignment and sentencing. It also included the testimony of police officers in a language that usually reflected their culture outside the courtroom.

5. *The languages of the alcoholism treatment center.* The staff at the center came from three distinct cultural scenes: social work, law enforcement, and Alcoholics Anonymous. In order to carry out their tasks, staff members frequently translated their meanings into terms the others could understand. However, their distinct language usages emerged in almost every conversation. For example, a social worker would refer to tramps as "patients," a guard from the Sheriff's Department would call them "inmates," and an alcoholic counselor would call them "alcoholics." Each term conveyed a distinct meaning with enormous implications for the tramps assigned to the treatment center.

Although this research situation may appear linguistically complex, even in the simplest situations, ethnographers must deal with their own language and that of informants. More important, they must deal with their own tendency to translate and simplify. I want to suggest three principles for you to keep in mind when making an ethnographic record: (a) the language identification principle, (b) the verbatim principle, and (c) the concrete principle. These principles have a single purpose, to create a more accurate ethnographic record and one that will facilitate ethnographic analysis. Let us look at each briefly.

The Language Identification Principle

This principle can be simply stated: *identify the language used for each fieldnote entry.* Whenever you write something down in your fieldnotes, because it is necessary to select a language, some method of identification must be used. This might involve setting things off in parentheses, quotation marks, or brackets. It must include identification of the speaker. The goal is to have an ethnographic record *that reflects the same differences in language usages as the actual field situation.*

When I first began fieldwork on skid row, I failed to follow the language identification principle. My record of events was recorded in what I call an "amalgamated language," which included a mixture of terms and usages picked up from tramps, from the languages in the courtroom, from the treatment center staff, and still others drawn from my own enculturation (Figure 10). From long discussions with other ethnographers, I have found that this is not an uncommon experience. Ethnographers tend to fall back on creating an amalgamated language, taking the things spoken by others and rephrasing them into a composite picture of the cultural scene.

The use of an amalgamated language for recording fieldnotes has the apparent virtue of simplification. However, when the ethnographer returns to these notes to make a more careful analysis of cultural meanings, it becomes difficult if not impossible to do. Cultural meanings have become distorted during the process of making an ethnographic record.

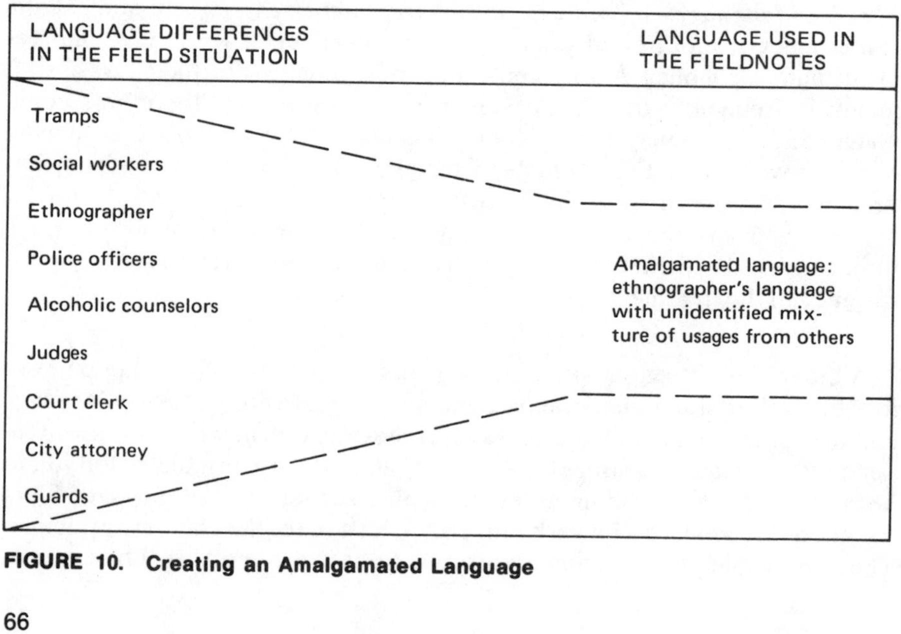

FIGURE 10. Creating an Amalgamated Language

The Verbatim Principle

In addition to identifying the various language usages in the field situation, the ethnographer must *make a verbatim record of what people say*. This obvious principle of getting things down word-for-word is frequently violated. Whether recording things people say in natural contexts or in more formal ethnographic interviews, the investigator's tendency to translate continues to operate. When I began research with tramps I did not realize the importance of the verbatim principle and freely summarized, restated, and condensed what informants said without realizing it.

Consider the following example.

Informant's actual statement: "I made the bucket in Seattle one time for pooling; I asked a guy how much he was holding on a jug and he turned out to be a ragpicker and he pinched me."

Fieldnote entry: "I talked to Joe about his experience of being arrested on skid row when he wasn't drunk."

At the time, this condensed entry appeared sufficient; I certainly did not feel it was a distortion of what Joe said. I didn't fully understand all his words but I thought I knew roughly what they meant. However, this entry lost some of the most important clues to the informant's culture, clues that came from such folk terms as *pooling* (a complex routine for contributing to a fund for purchasing something), *the bucket* (city jail), *ragpicker* (a certain kind of policeman), and *pinched* (arrested). Joe's phrases were leads to further questions; my summary was not. As my research progressed, I became aware that the words informants spoke held one key to their culture and so I began to make a verbatim record.

It may seem wiser, under the pressure of an interview situation or in some natural context, to make a quick and more complete summary rather than a partial verbatim record. Such is not the case. In the previous example it would have been more valuable to make a partial, but verbatim record such as the following:

"made the bucket"
"holding on a jug"
"a ragpicker . . . pinched me"

These scattered phrases could then have been used to generate ethnographic questions; the summary could not.

Both *native terms* and *observer terms* will find their way into the fieldnotes. The important thing is to carefully distinguish them. The native terms must be recorded verbatim. Failure to take these first steps along the path to discovering the inner meaning of another culture will lead to a false confidence that we have found out what the natives know. We may never even realize that our picture is seriously distorted and incomplete.

The Concrete Principle

This principle states, *when describing observations, use concrete language*. In studying a head start program for preschool children, Dixon recorded the following concrete description:

Walking back from the park, Tammy and DeeDee were holding Aleisha's hand, and began to dig their nails into her hand, she started crying, they let go and she clung to my hand crying; this was getting a little awkward, I was holding Vivian's coat and her hand; Audrey was semiwrapped around my leg; and Aleisha on the other hand, and the coat was slipping but I couldn't get free enough to get it more firmly over my arm. . . . Vivian then tried digging her nails into my hand to see if it could hurt, luckily they're short and didn't so I didn't react at all, like I didn't even notice, and she stopped (1972:207).

Consider how easy it is to use generalities instead of concrete description. Dixon could have simply said, "The children fought for my attention on the way home." "The children" instead of Tammy and DeeDee and Aleisha and Vivian and Audrey. "Fought" instead of digging nails, crying, holding, clinging, and wrapping around legs. "For my attention" rather than describing the actions of each child and her own reactions.

Writing in concrete language is difficult because most people have had years of training to condense, summarize, abbreviate, and generalize. We have learned to avoid writing that is "too wordy." In writing up fieldnotes we must reverse this deeply ingrained habit of generalization and *expand, fill out, enlarge,* and give as much *specific detail* as possible.

One way to help expand the concrete language of description in taking fieldnotes is to make lists of verbs and nouns which can be expanded later. For example, let's say you made observations of people standing in line and listed these verbs: *standing, shifting, looking up, looking down, searching pockets, wagging head, nodding head, scratching, glaring, raising eyebrows, backing up, beelining, walking.* This would enhance a concrete description in your fieldnotes. If you observed people walking their dogs in a park, you could list nouns like *chain leash, leather leash, dirt path, sidewalk, curb, asphalt path, leaves, grass, fire plug, tree, stick, purse, coats,* and so on.

In following this principle of using concrete language, the ethnographer must guard against the tendency to allow the abstract jargon of social science to creep into descriptive fieldnotes. A major goal of social science is to generalize. Words like *role, hostility, withdrawal, social interaction, ceremony, actor, social situation, cultural strategy, socialization, giving support, communicating,* and *observing* are all generalizations. Although you will want to make generalizations during your research, it is necessary to begin with concrete facts that you see, hear, taste, smell, and feel. If your fieldnotes become filled with the abstract jargon of social science, you will find it difficult to make generalizations from these generalizations. In doing ethnography every ethnographer must learn to shift back and forth between the concrete language of description and the more abstract language of generalization. By maintaining a strict separation, especially when taking fieldnotes, you will add depth and substance to your study.

KINDS OF FIELDNOTES

There are several different kinds of fieldnotes that make up an ethnographic record. Every ethnographer develops a system for organizing a file and field notebook. The following suggested format reflects the organization I have found most useful.

The Condensed Account

All notes taken during actual field observations represent a condensed version of what actually occurred. It is humanly impossible to write down everything that goes on or everything informants say. Condensed accounts often include phrases, single words, and unconnected sentences. Consider the experience of one ethnographer who decided to interview a policeman. After making contact, her informant wanted her to ride in the squad car for a four-hour shift. In the squad car, she began to make notes of things that occurred, the places they drove, calls that came over the radio, and many of the phrases and terms used by her informant. During the four hours she recorded several pages of *condensed notes* in her notebook. She left the first interview with a feeling that she had recorded only a tiny bit of what she had experienced. Still, this condensed account was of enormous value because it had been recorded on the spot.

It is advisable to make a condensed account during every period of fieldwork or immediately afterward. In his study of pinball players, Sanders writes:

Because it was an unobtrusive study and I could find no way to take notes in the setting without drawing attention to myself, I waited until I returned home to write up the findings. It was a five-minute walk from where I lived to the poolhall; thus, there was a minimum amount that was forgotten or left out. Observation time lasted from fifteen minutes to an hour and a half, covering all days of the week and all hours that the establishment was open for business (1973).

Under such conditions, condensed notes may still be the best way to quickly record key phrases and to identify major events. If you decided not to take

69

notes in the social situation you are observing, try to find a convenient place nearby where you can at least make condensed notes *immediately following* each observation. If you must spend an hour driving from your fieldwork site, take time to make condensed notes before making that drive. The sooner you record your observations the more vivid and detailed your account. The real value of a condensed account comes when it is expanded after completing an interview or field observation.

The Expanded Account

The second type of fieldnotes represents an expansion of the condensed version. As soon as possible after each field session (or after making a condensed account), the ethnographer should fill in details and recall things that were not recorded on the spot. The key words and phrases jotted down can serve as useful reminders to create the expanded account. When expanding, keep in mind the language identification principle, the verbatim principle, and the concrete principle.

Much of my research among skid row men took place at the alcoholism treatment center where I mingled informally with informants while they worked, ate, played cards, and sat around talking. Occasionally, I jotted down condensed notes on small cards carried in my pocket. After several hours of listening and watching, I would slip away to a private office and expand my notes with as many details as I could remember. Like most ethnographers, I discovered my ability to recall events and conversations increased rapidly through the discipline of creating expanded accounts from condensed ones.

On each return visit to a research setting the ethnographer observes activities that appear similar, if not identical, to what occurred earlier. If you select a social situation with an eye to *recurrent events,* the repetition quickly becomes evident. When making expanded notes it becomes all too easy to skip over things seen and recorded previously, feeling "I've already described that in my fieldnotes." Instead of avoiding repetition, the ethnographer welcomes it as one of the best clues to the culture. The descriptions in your fieldnotes should reflect the actual field situation. If events and activities occur over and over again, you will need to describe them over and over again.

Repetition, both of field observations and concrete descriptions in your fieldnotes, is one of the surest ways to overcome what I call the "tip-of-the-iceberg assumption." Almost everyone, beginning ethnographer or experienced fieldworker, experiences the feeling that "not much is going on" in a new social situation. Especially when doing micro-ethnography, we fall prey to this assumption. We mistake the tip of the iceberg for the entire mountain of ice, nine-tenths of which lies hidden beneath the ocean surface. Only through repeated observations and repeated descriptions in fieldnotes does the ethnographer begin to see the complexity of a seemingly simple social situation.

I recall the experience of Frank (1976), a student ethnographer who decided to study the way other students crossed a street that separates the main campus of Macalester College from several dormitories and the student cafeteria. At first, this social situation appeared quite simple, hardly worth studying. Students stepped off the curb, walked across the street while watching for oncoming cars, and stepped up on the opposite curb. Setting aside the tip-of-the-iceberg assumption, Frank found an observation post and began making repeated entries, describing in concrete language what she saw. She crossed the street herself under many different conditions. Each day it seemed that she was recording the same things. Then, after a few weeks, some interesting patterns began to emerge and she began to see things she hadn't noticed at first.

She observed, for example, that crossing the street occurred in several complex stages, each with sets of cultural rules. Once she identified the stages, she discovered certain obstacles to carrying out the activities required of each stage. Then she discovered, from the way people behaved, that one of the goals was to cross the street without the embarrassment that comes from things like stumbling, waiting too long, being caught alone in the middle, or even making all the traffic stop. Crossing the street was indeed a social situation, a stage on which actors played the roles they had learned. And several patterns emerged in the way people crossed. She identified four types: *the careful planner, the impatient edger, the lane-by-laner,* and *the overcautious pessimist.* Through patient and repeated observations she discussed the tacit cultural rules for a common urban activity, crossing a street. Had she given in to the assumption that the tip of the iceberg was the entire iceberg, it would have influenced her observations, fieldnotes, and eventually the quality of her research.

A Fieldwork Journal

In addition to fieldnotes that come directly from observing and interviewing (the condensed account and expanded account), ethnographers should always keep a journal. Like a diary, this journal will contain a record of experiences, ideas, fears, mistakes, confusions, breakthroughs, and problems that arise during fieldwork. A journal represents the personal side of fieldwork; it includes reactions to informants and the feelings you sense from others.

Each journal entry should be dated. Rereading your journal at a later time will reveal how quickly you forget what occurred during the first days and weeks of fieldwork. Months later, when you begin to write up the study, the journal becomes an important source of data. Doing ethnography differs from many other kinds of research in that you, the ethnographer, become a major research instrument. Making an introspective record of fieldwork enables a person to take into account personal biases and feelings, to understand their influences on the research.

Analysis and Interpretation

The fourth type of fieldnotes provides a link between the ethnographic record and the final written ethnography. Here is the place to record generalizations, analyses of cultural meanings, interpretations, and insights into the culture studied. Most of the tasks in the remaining steps involve detailed analysis of your fieldnotes and can be recorded in this category of fieldnotes.

Analysis and interpretation notes often represent a kind of brainstorming. Ideas may come from past reading, from some particular theoretical perspective, from some comment made by an informant, from talking about your project with a friend. It is important to think of this section in your fieldwork notebook as a place to "think on paper" about the culture under consideration.

Tasks

3.1 Set up a fieldwork notebook or file with sections for
   a. condensed accounts.
   b. expanded accounts.
   c. a journal.
   d. analysis and interpretation.
3.2 Conduct a period of participant observation and record your experience.
3.3 Select one paragraph of expanded fieldnotes and, using more concrete language, try to expand it into several paragraphs.

OBJECTIVES
1. To learn to make descriptive observations.
2. To identify the different kinds of descriptive observations.
3. To conduct a period of participant observation for the purpose of making descriptive observations.

By now your have conducted at least one session of field-work and made some observations. Every day you spend in the field from now on will involve making more observations. At first, many ethnographers feel overwhelmed with all the things to be observed and recorded. In particular, you may be wondering, "Am I observing the things that I should be, the things that are important?" Each ethnographer must discover the answer to that question and the answer will change during the course of fieldwork. The most useful thing at this point is to gain a better understanding of observation itself and the various types to use. In this step we shall examine the first and most important type, *descriptive observation*.

You will make descriptive observations whenever you look at a social situation and try to record as much as possible. It means approaching the activity in process without any *particular* question in mind, but only the *general* question, "What is going on here?" In Chapter Three of Part One, I identified the three major types of observation and discussed their sequence in fieldwork. As we focus on descriptive observation in this chapter, keep in mind that you will learn the other types in this progression:

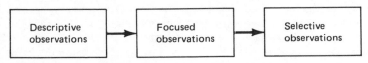

Underlying each of these forms of observation is a mode of inquiry based on asking questions.

THE ETHNOGRAPHIC INQUIRY UNIT

The basic unit of all ethnographic inquiry is the *question-observation*. Neither exists in isolation from the other. We examined this proposition at some length in our earlier discussion of the ethnographic research cycle. Now, as you are in the field making observations, you need to keep in mind that each thing you see and record is influenced by the questions you have in mind. You will gain skill in observing as you gain skill in asking the right questions.

Let's consider an actual fieldwork case. Several years ago I was assigned to a grand jury and decided to use the opportunity to conduct ethnographic fieldwork. I worked unobtrusively, participating as a member of the grand jury, making notes during meetings when possible, and recording my observations in more developed form after a day-long session. Here are some of my fieldnotes made during the first meeting.

I parked near the county courthouse and walked the short distance to the new building. Streams of people flowed into the lobby and scrambled into the waiting doors of elevators. "Going up sir?" a young man called to me from one of the eight elevators. I nodded, stepped in, and waited until he stopped at the eighth floor where I knew the Marshall County Criminal Court was located.

I followed the hallway until I saw a sign over two large doors: CRIMINAL COURT. I decided to go in even though there was still five minutes before the appointed hour of 9:00 A.M. I pushed open one of the swinging doors and found myself in a large courtroom.

There were rows of spectator benches, all made of heavy dark wood, oak or walnut, to match the paneled walls. The rows of benches went for more than twenty-five feet until they met a railing that seemed to neatly mark off a large area for "official business." I went in, sat down in the last row of spectators' benches, and looked around at the few other people seated at various places in the courtroom. The high ceiling and heavy dark wood made me feel as if I were in a sacred, almost religious place. Two people sitting in front of me were talking in hushed tones and I could not hear what they said. As newcomers came in, they would stop, look around, and then move very slowly to find a place to sit. At the right of the area behind the railing were twelve high-back leather chairs behind another railing. A large oak table with massive chairs all faced toward a high lectern which I took to be the judge's bench. All this area was empty. I waited.

A few minutes after nine a man walked in with a brisk manner. He looked at the people scattered around the large courtroom, all of us in the spectators' area, and said, "Hello. I assume you are all here for the prospective grand jury. Judge Fred Adams is going to be on the bench and it would be better if you all sat in the jury box." Slowly people got up and I joined them as we moved together toward the front. How easy for some unknown man to give orders and we all obey. I took a seat in the front row and soon all twelve chairs were filled; several people sat in the first row of the spectators area; three men sat in chairs inside the area of "official business." I wondered if this was where we would meet for the next few months or what we would be called upon to do. I spoke to no one, although I could hear some comments being made quietly. I took out a tablet and began making fieldnotes. I wondered if the people around me thought I was writing a letter or what. I was conscious of standing out in my casual clothes and beard. All the others were dressed neatly; the men in suits and ties, some in sportcoats. Many dark business suits. They all looked professional. The women were well dressed in suits, dresses, high heels, make-up. All looked older than myself. It was as if they had all dressed for some formal occasion. I felt a little out of place, but decided that didn't matter.

The man who had called us to the jury box began calling out names. "Mrs. Mary Wendt." "Here." "How about Joseph Walters?" "Here." I wrote down as many names as I could, but they came so fast I missed some. "James P. Spradley?" he called out, clearly mispronouncing it. "Is that right?" he asked as I said, "Here." I nodded, trying not to call attention to the fact of my presence. He continued through the list, and as a few more people drifted in he read off their names also. Several people did not answer. No one seemed concerned or at least no one volunteered information about the missing persons.

I began to overhear people behind me talking. "It's fun to get into something new," a lady's voice said. "Yes, I like to have new experiences," came another voice. "Mine was in the mail when I returned from vacation." I think she was referring to the letter saying we had been selected for the grand jury. "I can't sleep in. I have insomnia. I couldn't get to sleep before two A.M. and I woke up at six so I only got four hours of sleep."

I wasn't sure what we were waiting for, but probably the judge. "I took two Gelusil this morning," came the voice of a different woman, obviously nervous. A man down the row rustled a newspaper he was reading. "I didn't know how many criminal courts there were but I figured the elevator operator would know where I was supposed to come." This was the first woman's voice. I glanced around. She was wearing a red dress. "I don't even know how many they send these things to." "It's twenty-three I think," came the voice of a man who had been listening to their conversation. "And they hope to get sixteen." There was an obvious air of expectation. I felt it. We had been chosen—and we didn't know how, or at least I didn't and some of the others didn't. But to be one of the select persons in this group with an interesting task; not knowing how long we would meet or what we would do—at the moment all seemed rather exciting.

The man who was reading our names was joined by a sheriff's officer in full uniform, gun mounted on his left hip. He walked across the courtroom and stood near a door near the high judge's bench. The man and the police officer kept looking at each other, one glanced at his watch, there was an air of expectancy in the jury box also. You could feel something important was about to happen, but I'm not sure how we knew.

"Will everyone rise!" The officer shouted his command at the exact instant that the door opened. "The court of Fred Adams, honorable judge of Marshall County, is now in session." [That is an approximation since I couldn't write while standing and I couldn't remember exactly what he said.] I stood at attention and felt my heart beating faster than usual. A tall, gray-headed man in full black robe walked slowly in, turned toward the bench, and went up and sat down. Everyone was completely attentive. The moment had arrived.

"You may sit down," he said, after sitting down himself and arranging his robe. "I want to give you some general instructions. I'm going to appoint one of your number as foreman. Mr. Stone, will you serve as foreman?" He spoke with authority, not asking a question, but giving an order. "Yes, your honor." Mr. Stone spoke quickly and quietly.

This rather lengthy record actually covers less than fifteen minutes of observation. It is entirely descriptive and one can quite easily see the *implied questions* I had in mind.

1. What did I do on the first day of the grand jury?
2. What is the courtroom like?
3. How did other prospective jurors, the judge, and other officials act on the first day?
4. What did people say?

These are all examples of *descriptive questions* that lead to *descriptive observations*. Obviously, I did not record other information that could have been observed that day, such as the color of each juror's shoes, the color of each man's tie, or the spacing distances among prospective jurors when they first took seats in the criminal courtroom. Such specific questions might emerge later as important. At this stage of any investigation, general descriptions were the first priority.

When ethnographers work with informants, they can ask descriptive questions to elicit the informant's observations of social situations. For example, if I wanted to compare the grand jury I participated on with others, I could locate informants and begin by asking these same questions: "What did you do on the first day of the grand jury?" and so on. In a sense, when you make descriptive observations, you participate in a social situation, then *treat yourself as an informant*. (See Spradley 1979 for a discussion of interviewing informants.)

Descriptive observations, in response to descriptive questions, will include a considerable amount of information about the ethnographer. First, it includes the ethnographer's actions. I described where I went, what I did, where I sat, how I overheard things, and who I saw. Description of any kind is always from some point of view. It originates in the sensory organs of some specific individual. Later I might want to make general statements about that first day on the grand jury, but for the present it is important to include my actions. Second, descriptions include the ethnographer's thoughts and feelings. As an individual I have access to my feelings and my thoughts. I can say, "I wondered if this is where we would meet . . .," and "I felt a little out of place. . . ."

Although there are an endless number of descriptive questions one can ask, it is helpful to classify them into types that give rise to specific types of descriptive observations.

KINDS OF DESCRIPTIVE OBSERVATIONS

A descriptive question-observation can occur even when the ethnographer has very little knowledge of a social situation. Indeed, they are designed to guide you in research when you are most ignorant of the culture under consideration. Almost all such observations can be reduced to two major types: grand tour observations and mini-tour observations.

Grand Tour Observations

The concept of "grand tour" comes from the common experience of having someone show us around their house, place of business, or school. Friends come for dinner, and as they stand in the entrance to my home they say, "My, what a nice place you have." "Would you like to see the rest of the house?" I ask politely. "Sure, that would be great." And as we begin the route from one room to another, I comment, "Okay, I'll give you a grand tour." What follows is an identification of the *major features* of my home. I'll point out that the kitchen has been remodeled; I will identify the laundry room and the study. However, I will not discuss the cost of remodeling the kitchen or go into detail about all the activities that go on in the laundry room or study.

Later, on that first day the grand jury began its work, we moved to what was called "the grand jury room." "Can you describe the grand jury room?" This question led to a grand tour description which included the features someone would encounter if they entered the room, walked around in the room, and investigated the objects in the room.

We can expand the idea of a grand tour to include almost every aspect of experience in addition to spatial location. Let's take the largest sequence of events in the grand jury. "Can you describe the major things that take place when you are on a grand jury, from the first moment you learn about it until it is all over?" The following entry offers an abbreviated response to this question and will give you a grand tour of these events over time.

Serving on the grand jury begins when you receive a letter that informs you that you have been selected and must appear on a certain date. This is followed by a period of waiting, and for most jurors wondering what will be entailed. Some make phone calls to the Marshall County Courthouse to find out more information or to try and be excused from duty.

The next major event takes place when the prospective jurors appear in a courtroom and receive instructions about the legal duties of a grand jury. The judge read this to us from the statute book and then we were sworn in. We had to take an oath that we would perform our duty and abide by the laws.

This was followed on the same day by the first meeting in the grand jury room. At this meeting the Marshall County prosecuting attorney explained what the group was supposed to do, how he would bring cases, and maybe some witnesses, and then we had to vote as to whether there was enough evidence to have a regular case. We heard a couple of cases that first day. Actually, the day was broken up into hearing cases presented, discussing the cases, taking coffee breaks, taking a lunch break, then hearing more cases, and finally leaving.

After monthly meetings for three months, another event took place when we went out to investigate the jails. The grand jury has the authority to see if the jails are being run according to the law and that no prisoners' rights are being violated. We divided up into smaller groups and visited the jails. Then there was the last meeting, and some weeks later each juror received a check for gasoline and salary of six dollars per day.

Like all grand tour observations, this one provides only the most general features of these events. It gives an overview of what occurred.

In an earlier step we identified three major features of all social situations: *place, actor,* and *activities,* each of which provides a possible grand tour description. For example, in the grand jury setting I tried to describe the various actors involved. Among these were the *judge, county attorney, assistant county attorney, bailiff, witnesses, defendants, jurors,* and on one occasion an *interpreter*. There were numerous witnesses and jurors, thus offering room for a grand tour description of all the different types within each of these categories.

In addition to these three features of social situations, we can now identify six more that will help you in formulating initial grand tour questions and making the observations. This will give a total of nine major dimensions of every social situation.

1. *Space*: the physical place or places
2. *Actor*: the people involved
3. *Activity*: a set of related acts people do
4. *Object*: the physical things that are present
5. *Act*: single actions that people do
6. *Event*: a set of related activities that people carry out
7. *Time*: the sequencing that takes place over time
8. *Goal*: the things people are trying to accomplish
9. *Feeling*: the emotions felt and expressed

In a most general sense, these dimensions can serve as guides for the participant observer. Consider the dimension of time, for example. I have already sketched in an overview of the sequence of events from the perspective of a grand juror. In addition, each meeting lasted most of a single day and the events were scheduled over time in a particular way. Every social situation includes this temporal dimension and by focusing on this dimension, new observations emerge. In the grand jury, cases heard at the beginning of the day frequently moved slower than cases heard toward the end of the day. This difference in *tempo* could be described not only for cases but for other activities as well.

After making numerous notes on the meetings and the specifics of cases, I realized that the dimension of *feeling* had been largely ignored. The question, "What are all the different feelings people have during grand jury meetings?" could lead to new and important grand tour observations. "What are all the goals people seem to be trying to achieve?" was equally revealing when one considered all the different people who participated in the grand jury process. These nine dimensions are not equally important for every social situation, but they do provide the beginning ethnographer with an excellent guide for making grand tour observations.

Mini-tour Observations

Almost all participant observation begins with grand tour observations. The descriptions entered in your fieldnotes offer almost unlimited opportunities for investigating smaller aspects of experience. Because grand tour observations lead to such rich descriptions of a social situation, the ethnographer must guard against the feeling, "I've described everything in this social situation." Every grand tour observation is like a large room with numerous doors into smaller rooms, each door to be opened by a mini-tour question-observation.

The form taken by mini-tour questions is identical to the questions that lead to grand tour observations except that mini-tour questions deal with a much smaller unit of experience. In asking yourself either type of question, you will always begin with phrases like the following:

1. What are all the . . . (places, acts, events, feelings, and the like)
2. Can you describe in detail the . . . (objects, times, goals, and the like)
3. Can you tell me about all the . . . (people, activities, and the like)

The second part of each question that leads to a mini-tour observation draws on specific information already discovered. Let's go back to the grand jury and see how to make mini-tour observations.

Earlier in this chapter I presented a grand tour of the major events that occurred over time on the grand jury, from the first moment a juror received notification until the last contact with the Marshall County Court. Here are some questions that guided me in making mini-tour observations:

1. Can you describe the period of waiting for the first meeting of the grand jury, what goes through your mind, what people do, and how they feel?
2. Can you describe in detail the first time the prospective jurors met in the criminal courtroom and received instructions from the judge?
3. Can you tell me all about a single case from the moment it is introduced by the prosecuting attorney until it is completely over?
4. What goes on during the coffee break? What are all the things people do in the order they do them?
5. Can you tell me in detail what happens during the time before the grand jury meetings begin, from the moment the first person arrives until the last one comes in and the meeting begins?

Here is the beginning of a lengthy fieldnote entry in response to the mini-tour question about a single case.

There was an air of anticipation, a few minutes during which the members of the grand jury sat in silence and the prosecuting attorney searched through his files. Then he said, "I've got two cases to present this morning. I'll have to rush. We have ten witnesses." He spoke fast and conveyed a strong impression that we would have to move quickly throughout the morning.

"This is a case of felonious theft by retention. It means retaining property of at least $2500, retail market value on the date of the offense. Here is a summary of the case. One day in July a van was broken into and a revolver was stolen. Then later there was another robbery of stereo equipment from a stereo store. The police, making an investigation of a house, recovered the revolver, three Pioneer receivers, one Teac tape deck, two JBL speakers. There were three people in the house at the time, and the police found the prints of one of them on some of the stereo equipment."

The prosecuting attorney spoke rapidly, and when he came to this point he looked up at a clerical assistant and motioned to him. He got up and left the grand jury room. I looked at the people on the grand jury and they were now whispering to each other, all looked very interested.

"We now have our first witness," the prosecuting attorney said as the clerk returned with a middle-aged man dressed in a blue business suit. The clerk pointed to a chair, the man sat down, the clerk asked him to raise his hand and proceeded to administer an oath: "Do you swear to tell the truth, the whole truth, and nothing but the truth, so help you God?" "I do."

"What is your name?" the prosecuting attorney asked. "Bob Johnson." "Would you spell your name and give your address?" "B-O-B J-O-H-N-S-O-N, 42 East Alder, Center City."

"On July 14 did you report a theft?"

"Yes, a .38 Colt was stolen from my van. I had purchased it in February of 1972, paid $118 for it. At the time I worked for the Center City Police Department and I have a permit to carry the revolver."

"As of July 10, do you have any opinion about the retail value of the .38 Colt?"

"Yes. About $140 because it had gone up about $20 more than the purchase price."

The prosecuting attorney turned abruptly to the grand jury and asked: "Any questions?" He paused for a total of three seconds, turned to the witness, and said, "Okay" and the clerk quickly ushered him out of the grand jury room.

You can see from this partial example how mini-tour observations lead to an enormous number of detailed descriptions. Your goal in making this kind of observation is to take what sometimes appears as a trivial event, such as a coffee break, and record it in concrete detail.

DESCRIPTIVE QUESTION MATRIX

The number of questions you can formulate to lead you to grand tour and mini-tour observations is almost limitless. By selecting each of the nine dimensions of social situations in turn, you can describe most features of any social situation. As you consider these dimensions such as space, actors, feelings, and goals, you will discover that your questions tend to lead you to the way these dimensions are *interrelated*. For example, you might begin with a grand tour question like, "What are the major *events* in this social situation?" Then you might ask, "Who are all the *actors* in this social situation?" Then it would be possible to ask several mini-tour questions that *relate* these two dimensions such as:

1. Which actors participate in which events?
2. In what ways do events change relationships among actors?

As a guide to asking grand tour and mini-tour questions I have found it useful to prepare a matrix with each of the nine dimensions listed along both axes of the matrix. With such a matrix you can formulate descriptive questions for all the relationships possible among the nine dimensions of social situations. I have prepared a sample matrix which includes nine grand tour questions in the set of diagonal boxes and a great many mini-tour questions in all the other boxes of the matrix. The exact form of these questions will change from one social situation to another, but they can be used as a guide for checking your own thoroughness. It should be kept in mind that each social situation is different; each will emphasize some dimensions more than others. For example, in studying the grand jury I had very few *objects* to describe. Much of my time was spent observing one particular kind of *activity:* speaking. In another fieldwork project in a factory that produced equipment for tanneries, much of the description involved *objects*. This descriptive question matrix is offered as a guide to making descriptive observations. Each person who uses it will have to adapt it to the social situation under investigation. You will find yourself asking more questions from one part of the matrix than from others. However, by checking against this type of matrix you can avoid the problem of overlooking important ethnographic data.

In this step we have discussed the first type of observation made by ethnographers doing fieldwork. Although you will move to other types in the future, you will continue to make descriptive observations during part of every fieldwork period.

In commencing fieldwork the ethnographer is like a map-maker who sets foot on an uncharted island. Because the terrain is *unknown,* the map-maker cannot set out to locate deposits of iron ore, lakes, volcanoes, and landslides caused by earthquakes. At the start of the investigation one does not even know if these physical features exist. Instead of beginning with preconceived ideas about what to find, the map-maker sets out to describe what can be observed. Whatever the individual encounters goes into the record book. Certainly this kind of investigator will overlook some important features of the landscape, but later, after a preliminary survey map has been drawn, it will be possible to come back to the island to discover and include more details. In much the same way, the ethnographer begins with descriptive observations stimulated by grand tour questions. At almost the same time, with

Descriptive Question Matrix

	SPACE	OBJECT	ACT	ACTIVITY
SPACE	Can you describe in detail all the *places*?	What are all the ways space is organized by objects?	What are all the ways space is organized by acts?	What are all the ways space is organized by activities?
OBJECT	Where are objects located?	Can you describe in detail all the *objects*?	What are all the ways objects are used in acts?	What are all the ways objects are used in activities?
ACT	Where do acts occur?	How do acts incorporate the use of objects?	Can you describe in detail all the *acts*?	How are acts a part of activities?
ACTIVITY	What are all the places activities occur?	What are all the ways activities incorporate objects?	What are all the ways activities incorporate acts?	Can you describe in detail all the *activities*?
EVENT	What are all the places events occur?	What are all the ways events incorporate objects?	What are all the ways events incorporate acts?	What are all the ways events incorporate activities?
TIME	Where do time periods occur?	What are all the ways time affects objects?	How do acts fall into time periods?	How do activities fall into time periods?
ACTOR	Where do actors place themselves?	What are all the ways actors use objects?	What are all the ways actors use acts?	How are actors involved in activities?
GOAL	Where are goals sought and achieved?	What are all the ways goals involve use of objects?	What are all the ways goals involve acts?	What activities are goal seeking or linked to goals?
FEELING	Where do the various feeling states occur?	What feelings lead to the use of what objects?	What are all the ways feelings affect acts?	What are all the ways feelings affect activities?

EVENT	TIME	ACTOR	GOAL	FEELING
What are all the ways space is organized by events?	What spatial changes occur over time?	What are all the ways space is used by actors?	What are all the ways space is related to goals?	What places are associated with feelings?
What are all the ways that objects are used in events?	How are objects used at different times?	What are all the ways objects are used by actors?	How are objects used in seeking goals?	What are all the ways objects evoke feelings?
How are acts a part of events?	How do acts vary over time?	What are the ways acts are performed by actors?	What are all the ways acts are related to goals?	What are all the ways acts are linked to feelings?
What are all the ways activities are part of events?	How do activities vary at different times?	What are all the ways activities involve actors?	What are all the ways activities involve goals?	How do activities involve feelings?
Can you describe in detail all the *events*?	How do events occur over time? Is there any sequencing?	How do events involve the various actors?	How are events related to goals?	How do events involve feelings?
How do events fall into time periods?	Can you describe in detail all the *time periods*?	When are all the times actors are "on stage"?	How are goals related to time periods?	When are feelings evoked?
How are actors involved in events?	How do actors change over time or at different times?	Can you describe in detail all the *actors*?	Which actors are linked to which goals?	What are the feelings experienced by actors?
What are all the ways events are linked to goals?	Which goals are scheduled for which times?	How do the various goals affect the various actors?	Can you describe in detail all the *goals*?	What are all the ways goals evoke feelings?
What are all the ways feelings affect events?	How are feelings related to various time periods?	What are all the ways feelings involve actors?	What are the ways feelings influence goals?	Can you describe in detail all the *feelings*?

mini-tour questions in mind, the ethnographer will observe and record the details of social life. As time goes on, each ethnographer will come back to events and activities observed earlier and try to describe them in more detail.

Once a map-maker or geographer has an initial description of an uncharted island, he or she might want to begin looking for specific relationships between land features. It might be possible to formulate some hypotheses to be tested by later observations. But before this can occur, the geographer will have to sit down with the maps and analyze them in great detail. In similar fashion, before you can go on to making focused and selected observations, you will need to analyze the data you have collected from making descriptive observations. In the next two steps we will examine ways you can analyze the data you have collected.

Tasks

4.1 Write out a series of questions that will lead to both grand tour observations and mini-tour observations. Review earlier fieldnotes to do so.

4.2 With these questions in mind, conduct a period of participant observation in which you make both grand tour observations and mini-tour observations.

4.3 Write up an expanded account of these descriptive observations.

OBJECTIVES
1. To understand the nature of ethnographic analysis.
2. To understand the nature of cultural domains.
3. To identify the steps in making a domain analysis.
4. To carry out a systematic domain analysis on all fieldnote descriptions collected to date.

By now you have collected and recorded many pages of descriptive observations in your fieldnotes. With grand tour and mini-tour questions in mind you could probably go on making more observations for many weeks. In fact, it would be possible to make *only* descriptive observations, describing in more and more detail the social situation you have selected. Some beginning ethnographers who work without guidance continue to collect descriptive observations until they decide it is time to write up their ethnographic report. Although many good ethnographies have been done this way, it is both time consuming and ineffective. In order to discover the cultural patterns of any social situation, you must undertake an intensive analysis of your data *before* proceeding further. You will recall our earlier discussion of the ethnographic research cycle which went from asking questions to collecting data to making an ethnographic record to *analyzing ethnographic data*. Only when you have completed the cycle will you be ready to return to the first step of asking more questions and then collecting more data. In this step we will examine the nature of ethnographic analysis and discuss in detail the first type: domain analysis.

ETHNOGRAPHIC ANALYSIS

Analysis of any kind involves a way of thinking. It refers to the systematic examination of something to determine its parts, the relationship among parts, and their relationship to the whole. Analysis is a search for *patterns*. In the social situation you are studying you have observed behavior and artifacts. As you have recorded what people do and say, you have been able to make inferences about what they know. But, in order to move on and describe the *cultural* behavior, the *cultural* artifacts, and the *cultural* knowledge, you must discover the patterns that exist in your data. In a general sense, all your ethnographic analysis will involve searching through your fieldnotes to discover cultural patterns.

85

Cultural Patterns and Social Situations

There is an important difference between the concept of *culture* and the concept of *social situation*. Social situation refers to the stream of behavior (activities) carried out by people (actors) in a particular location (place). As an ethnographer you are directly exposed to a social situation. You watch people crossing streets, lining up at bank windows, taking care of children at a day-care center, or engage in discussions in a grand jury room. A social situation is observable and something in which you can participate.

Culture, on the other hand, refers to the *patterns* of behavior, artifacts, and knowledge that people have learned or created. Culture is an organization of things, the meaning given by people to objects, places, and activities. *Every human society is culturally constituted.* As outsiders, ethnographers participate, observe, and ask questions to discover the cultural meanings known to insiders. Analysis of your fieldnotes is the first step in going beyond mere descriptions of behavior and things to discovering the cultural meaning of that behavior and all the things you see.

Consider the following line drawing of a social situation.

A description of this situation might read as follows. Two individuals are seated on wooden objects. They are facing each other; between them is a larger wooden platform on four legs. The wooden platform comes to the level of their chests; on the platform are several objects. The individuals incline their heads slightly toward the objects directly in front of them. Occasionally they move their hands, manipulating all or part of each object in front of them. Their feet rest on the floor, but occasionally they shift their feet from one position to another. Each individual is clothed. Sometimes their eyes are focused on each other or on more distant objects.

This description, made by a complete outsider, does not give many clues as to the *meaning of this social situation,* and it includes almost no *cultural information.* For example, through more participant observation and inquiry, an ethnographer might discover this social situation was culturally constituted in any of the following forms:

1. A religious bible study undertaken by two persons.
2. A job interview.
3. A psychological test.
4. A restaurant table, where two people are reading a menu.
5. A seance using holy books.
6. A place where two persons are preparing for a chess match.

You can probably think of other possibilities. Let's now culturally define this social situation by the following diagram:

SOCIAL SITUATION   CULTURAL MEANING

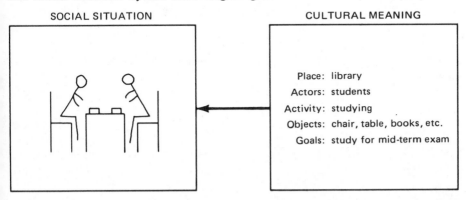

Place: library
Actors: students
Activity: studying
Objects: chair, table, books, etc.
Goals: study for mid-term exam

The stream of behavior represented in the line drawing has taken on meaning and organization. It has been defined. Culture is "the definition of the situation."

Now, it should be obvious that in your fieldnotes you have not been a completely ignorant outsider. You have already recorded many cultural meanings discovered through participant observation or known beforehand. Indeed, if you studied a library study table, it would be difficult to make and record descriptive observations without identifying some of the cultural meanings shown above. However, you cannot take these for granted without careful analysis and further observations. And if you study an unfamiliar social situation, you will find that much of what you see and hear has little meaning.

In this step I want to begin showing you how to systematically move from merely observing a *social situation* to discovering a *cultural scene,* two closely related but significantly different concepts. You first have to discover the *parts* or elements of cultural meaning and then find out how they are organized. We will begin with an important basic unit in every culture, the *cultural domain.* Domain analysis is the first type of ethnographic analysis. In later steps we will consider *taxonomic analysis,* which involves a search for the way cultural domains are organized, then *componential analysis,* which involves a search for the attributes of terms in each domain. Finally, we will consider *theme analysis,* which involves a search for the relationships among domains and for how they are linked to the cultural scene as a whole.

CULTURAL DOMAINS

A cultural domain is a category of cultural meaning that includes other smaller categories. Consider one type of actor that appeared before the members of the grand jury: *witnesses*. Once these people had been defined as witnesses, we on the grand jury no longer saw them merely as persons, but as a particular kind of person. "Witness" was a cultural category, a basic unit of cultural meaning in the context of grand juries. We knew it was a category of cultural meaning that included other smaller categories because the prosecuting attorney would say things like, "Now, we are going to hear from an *expert* witness," or "Now we will hear from a *defense* witness." "Kinds of witnesses" was one important cultural domain in this scene.

Consider an example of a cultural domain from another society. The category "friend" (*kabagayan*) in Tausug culture includes eight types of friends. This Philippine group described by Kiefer (1968) organizes people into the following types of "friends": ritual friend, close friend, casual friend, opponent, personal enemy, follower, ally, and neutral. "Kinds of friends" may be a domain in your culture, but it probably doesn't include all the types used by the Tausug. Note that they even include personal enemies in the category of friends, probably because through a special ceremony such enemies can be transformed into ritual friends.

Basic Elements of Cultural Domains

Cultural domains are categories of meaning. On the grand jury I was able to observe dozens of different witnesses, all of whom were unique in some way. However, we treated them all as if they were the same kind of person—witnesses. A category is an array of different objects that are treated as if they were equivalent. I will represent this "category" feature of all domains by the use of a box:

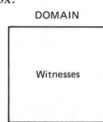

DOMAIN

Witnesses

Every culture creates hundreds of thousands of categories by taking unique things and classifying them together. Anything conceivable can be used to create such cultural categories, including eye blinks, ghosts, automobiles, dreams, clouds, and secret wishes. Domains, as cultural categories, are made up of three basic elements: *cover term, included terms,* and *semantic relationship.*

The cover term is the name for a cultural domain. "Witnesses" is the cover term for a domain from my data on the grand jury. "Friends" is a cover term for the Tausug domain mentioned earlier.

The included terms are the names for all the smaller categories inside the domain, such as "personal enemy," "ritual friend," and "opponent" in Tausug culture.

The third element in all cultural domains is a single semantic relationship, the linking together of two categories. As we shall see, semantic relationships are extremely important for discovering cultural domains. We can isolate one semantic relationship by stating the relationship of "personal enemies" and the domain "friend."

A personal enemy (is a kind of) friend. Here we see that two categories (personal enemy, friend) are linked by the semantic relationship -is a kind of-. We can now show these three elements in the following diagram:

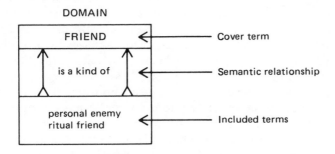

The semantic relationship operates on the general principle of *inclusion.* Its function is to define included terms by placing them *inside* the cultural domain.

Kinds of Domains

Any description of cultural domains always involves the use of language. Cover terms, included terms, and semantic relationships are all words and phrases that define and give meaning to the objects, events, and activities you observe. If you can record numerous samples of the way people talk you can use their *folk terms* to construct cultural domains. For example, in studying the grand jury I heard the prosecuting attorney say things like "expert witness," and "defense witness." At other times it becomes necessary to use your own terms to label what you see. Whenever you introduce words not in use by the people you are studying, we will call those *analytic terms,* a distinction that gives rise to three different kinds of domains.

1. Folk Domains. This domain occurs when all the terms come from the language used by people in the social situation. In his study of glider pilots, Rbyski (974) discovered several domains including types of *flights, gliders,* and *maneuvers.* The following folk domain is made up entirely of terms used by glider pilots.

MANEUVER		
	is a kind of	
take off	land	glide
turn	skid	slip
crab	spiral	chandelle
sideslip	stall	basic 8

2. Mixed domains. You may become interested in some domain for which there are only a few folk terms. Yet your observations clearly show that additional things exist which need labels. When this is the case you will want to select appropriate *analytic terms* to complete the domain. For example, in her study of runners, Northrop (1978) heard people use terms like "runner," "long-distance runner," and "track people." From observation it was clear that the cover term for the domain of people who used the indoor track was "runner." However, the other two folk terms did not account for all the variations in kinds of people who ran. For instance, some people visited the track only on rare occasions and didn't fit either of the categories. Northrop, on the basis of many observations and many hours of running herself, developed a mixed domain to categorize her discoveries.

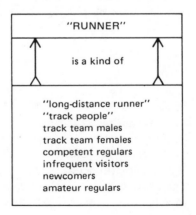

"RUNNER"	
	is a kind of
"long-distance runner"	
"track people"	
track team males	
track team females	
competent regulars	
infrequent visitors	
newcomers	
amateur regulars	

3. Analytic domains. Many of the cultural meanings remain tacit and you must infer them from what people do, what they say, and the artifacts they make and use. When a consistent pattern of cultural behavior emerges and you cannot discover any folk terms to label that behavior, you will need to select your own analytic terms. Consider the following example.

A common scene in most museums is a small group of people moving from one display to another. The group is often a family composed of one or more parents and several children. Hanson (1978) wanted to discover the cultural rules for using museums. She stationed herself in a large display room and observed group after group of family members coming and going. She also circulated through the museum taking fieldnotes on the behavior of people looking at the displays. Almost all the conversation she heard had to do with the museum artifacts on display. However, she became interested in the behavior of parents, a topic none of the family groups discussed. She began to observe every aspect of each group's behavior, how parents led the group of children, how they talked to the children, how they moved from one museum display to another, and everything else she could. Soon a number of patterns began to emerge, cultural patterns that suggested several appropriate styles parents could assume in leading their children through a museum. She identified the cover term "parent" and selected analytic terms for the domain she had discovered.

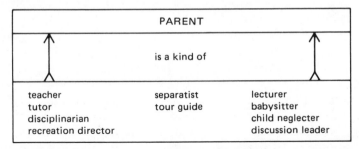

As you begin a domain analysis, keep in mind that you can start with either folk terms or analytic terms. Your goal is to discover the patterns of culture in a particular social situation. The first step is to identify possible domains. We now turn to the steps you can go through to make this kind of analysis.

STEPS IN MAKING A DOMAIN ANALYSIS

Let's go back to your fieldnotes for a moment. You have page after page of description, most of it in your own words, but here and there are folk terms you overheard. The cultural domains will not jump out at you from your fieldnotes. They are *embedded* in what you have already recorded. Your task is to search through the description for cover terms, included terms, and semantic relationships. Once you have found some part of a domain, you can use that as a tool for discovering more. Your fieldnotes are filled with an enormous number of cover terms and included terms. One good way to begin your analysis is to read over your fieldnotes, looking for *names for things,* including objects, places, people, and the like. Then, you can ask whether there are different *kinds* of these things. For example, at the beginning of the last step, I presented some fieldnotes from the first meeting of the grand jury. Looking over those notes, the following *possible cover terms* which are names for things emerged:

1. kinds of courthouses
2. kinds of jurors
3. kinds of judges
4. kinds of people
5. kinds of instructions
6. kinds of feelings

Another useful way to begin making a domain analysis makes use of the semantic relationship as a starting point. From a growing body of research, it appears that the number of semantic relationships in any culture is quite small, perhaps less than two dozen. In addition, certain semantic relationships appear to be universal. For instance, all cultures make use of what I shall call strict inclusion: "an oak (*is a kind of*) tree." These remarkable facts make semantic relationships an extremely important tool for ethnographic analysis. We will begin the steps in making a domain analysis with semantic relationships. At the same time, keep in mind that finding cultural domains is both science and art. Children in every society grow up and learn the domains of their culture without even knowing such a thing as a "domain" exists. At a young age they become "participant observers," watching others, listening to them, and slowly they learn to classify and code experience in the same way as adults. The steps in domain analysis presented below should not become a substitute for your own intuition and ingenuity.

There is another way to think about searching for domains that may be helpful. Perhaps you have seen a picture of a tree in which the artist has hidden several faces or animal figures. When you first look at the picture all you see is a tree. In fact, you might never guess that other figures were hidden among the branches and leaves without someone telling you. Then, knowing hidden faces are present you begin your search. It still appears to you like a tree and nothing more. Then suddenly you "see" a face or animal figure where before you had seen only leaves. Now your search takes on more interest; another one appears, then another. After such discoveries it becomes difficult to view the tree without also seeing the faces hidden in the drawing. Discovering cultural domains works in much the same way. You have already become familiar with your fieldnotes through writing them down. Now you will read them over again, this time searching for hidden domains among the leaves and branches. Once a domain is "discovered" you will find it easier to locate others and soon you will find it difficult to read your notes without seeing domains in every paragraph.

Step One: Select a single semantic relationship. In my own research and in working with other ethnographers, I have found the following universal semantic relationships the most useful for beginning an analysis of cultural domains. They are based on a number of important investigations into the universality of such relationships. For each one I will give an example from my study of the Marshall County Grand Jury.

RELATIONSHIP	FORM	EXAMPLE
1. Strict inclusion	X is a kind of Y	An expert witness (is a kind of) witness.
2. Spatial	X is a place in Y	The grand jury room (is a place in) the county courthouse.
	X is a part of Y	The jury box (is a part of) the criminal courtroom.
3. Cause-effect	X is a result of Y	Serving on the grand jury (is a result of) being selected.
4. Rationale	X is a reason for doing Y	A large number of cases (is a reason for) going rapidly.
5. Location-for-action	X is a place for doing Y	The grand jury room (is a place for) hearing cases.
6. Function	X is used for Y	Witnesses (are used for) bringing evidence.
7. Means-end	X is a way to do Y	Taking an oath (is a way to) symbolize the sacredness of jury duty.
8. Sequence	X is a step (stage) in Y	Making jail visits (is a stage in) grand jury activities.
9. Attribution	X is an attribution (characteristic) of Y	Authority (is an attribute of) the attorney.

It is possible to begin with any of these relationships or some other not listed that is important in your particular cultural scene. The two semantic relationships I suggest for making a start in domain analysis are *strict inclusion* (X is a kind of Y) and *means-end* (X is a way to Y). The former relationship focuses your attention on nouns, the latter on verbs. For purposes of illustration I will begin the analysis with strict inclusion.

Step Two: Prepare a domain analysis worksheet. Some ethnographers underline cover terms or semantic relationships directly in their fieldnotes or write in the margins to identify domains. I have found a separate worksheet a distinct advantage (Figure 11). You will need to go over your fieldnotes many times before you complete your research. By transferring your analysis to another sheet of paper, you will keep your fieldnotes from becoming cluttered with interpretations. A worksheet also helps to visualize the structure of each domain: cover term, included terms, semantic relationship.

1. Semantic Relationship: *Strict Inclusion*

2. Form: *X (is a kind of) Y.*

3. Example: *An oak (is a kind of) tree.*

Included Terms	Semantic Relationship	Cover Term
	IS A KIND OF	

Structural Questions: _____

Included Terms	Semantic Relationship	Cover Term
	IS A KIND OF	

Structural questions: _____

FIGURE 11. Domain Analysis Worksheet

Each domain analysis worksheet requires that you enter certain information before beginning the search: (1) the semantic relationship selected, (2) a statement of the form in which it is expressed, and (3) an example from your own culture of a sentence that has a cover term, an included term, and the semantic relationship (see Figure 11). The worksheet is divided into empty domains with blank spaces in which you enter the semantic relationship you have selected. Then, both cover term and the included terms will be written in as you identify them from your fieldnotes. Making systematic use of this kind of worksheet will help to uncover tacit domains embedded in the sentences you have written down earlier.

Step Three: Select a sample of fieldnote entries.   To begin with, one need only select a few paragraphs from the fieldnotes. Even shorter samples will do, although you will soon need to move on to the rest of your fieldnotes. Let's consider a selection from fieldnotes taken in a hospital:

Each day on the sixth floor of Fairview Hospital begins about eight when they bring breakfast to the patients. Two patients are in each room and the doctors visit about nine in the morning. Many patients feel helpless and they can't control things for themselves like the temperature in the rooms, getting what they want to eat, and getting enough sleep. Someone is always taking their temperature, changing an I.V., or bringing them food.

Perhaps the biggest problem expressed by patients is finding privacy. With two to a room one is exposed to the visitors of another patient who may crowd into your room, sit on your bed, and talk loudly. Loss of privacy seems to occur when other patients in the room will talk on the phone, sometimes for hours, will play the television, and will talk with his or her visitors. I observed several ways that patients try to achieve some small degree of privacy vis-à-vis the other patients as well as nurses. Some will pull the curtain that separates the two beds. Others will go for a walk in the hallways. It is possible, at a higher fee, to get a private room. A television lounge sits to the left of the nurses' station and some patients will sit in the lounge to escape the invasion of privacy from visitors to the other patient in their room.

Step Four: Search for possible cover terms and included terms that fit the semantic relationship.   This search involves reading, but reading in a particular manner. Instead of reading the meaning of sentences and focusing on their content, the ethnographer reads the fieldnotes with an eye for terms that might fit the semantic relationship. It means reading with a question in mind: "Which terms could be a kind of something?" or "Could there be different kinds of those?" Let's review the example above from a study of patients in a hospital, asking these questions. The following terms emerge as possible parts of one domain.

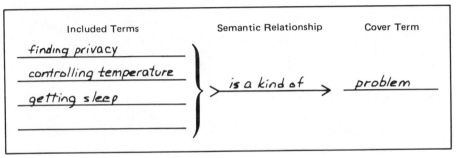

Included Terms	Semantic Relationship	Cover Term
finding privacy		
controlling temperature	is a kind of	problem
getting sleep		

Most of the time, especially when using small samples from your fieldnotes, only two or three included terms can be found for any domain. Indeed, sometimes only a single included term can be found. The number of included terms should not concern you. Your goal at this step is merely to identify cultural domains. Once you have identified the three basic elements, as in the example above, you can search for additional domains.

Let's look at another one from the fieldnotes above, still using the same semantic relationship.

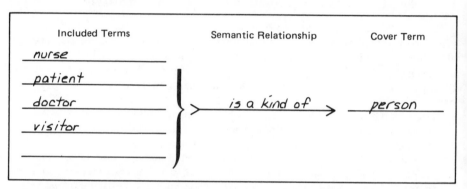

In this example we have taken a very brief description to use in our domain analysis. Our goal was to discover one or more domains using a single semantic relationship. Your task is much larger: you will need to go through all your fieldnotes with a single semantic relationship in mind. As you identify one domain, then move on to others, you will undoubtedly come across additional included terms. Record as many as you can find, but remember that your major goal is to compile a list of as many domains as possible.

Step Five: Repeat the search for domains using a different semantic relationship. For some of the semantic relationships I have identified you will find many domains; for others there will be relatively few. Let's look at one more example from the data on hospital patients, this time using the relationship of *means-end* (see page 97).

Some investigators find it useful to prepare their domain analysis worksheets on 4 × 6 cards, with a single domain for each card. As the list of included terms grows, it can be extended on the back of the card. As the stack of cards grows, the cards can be sorted easily into different piles and arranged to suit different purposes in analysis. Later, when the researcher begins writing up his or her ethnography, these cards become the source of organizing the description.

Step Six: Make a list of all identified domains. The goal of domain analysis is twofold. First, you are trying to identify cultural categories; second, you

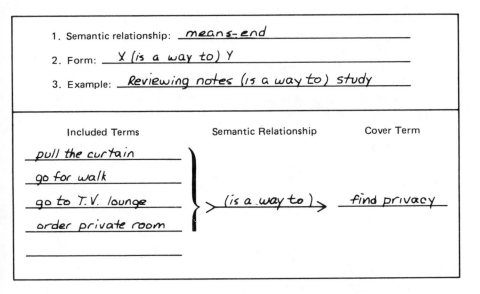

1. Semantic relationship: *means-end*

2. Form: *X (is a way to) Y*

3. Example: *Reviewing notes (is a way to) study*

Included Terms	Semantic Relationship	Cover Term
pull the curtain		
go for walk		
go to T.V. lounge	(is a way to)	find privacy
order private room		

want to gain an overview of the cultural scene you are studying. At first you may feel that there are an almost infinite number of cultural domains, that your task is endless. However, this is not the case. Beginning ethnographers who have carried out four or five hours of observation usually discover between twenty-five and two hundred cultural domains. It is not necessary to be completely exhaustive. With several dozen domains which represent most of the semantic relationships, you can achieve a good overview of the cultural scene.

Here is an example of a domain list from Hanson's study of parents and children in a museum (1978):

1. *X is a kind of Y*
   kinds of groups
   kinds of families
   kinds of attitudes
   kinds of postures
   kinds of relationships
   kinds of explanations
   kinds of questions kids ask

2. *X is a way to Y*
   ways to ask questions
   ways to compare things
   ways to describe museum artifacts
   ways parents try to teach children
   ways kids get parents' attention

ways to listen
ways kids teach each other
ways to have fun
ways to get parents to hurry up
ways to dress
ways to react to other visitors
ways to touch people
ways to ignore parents
ways kids act cool

3. *X is a part of Y*
   parts of an exhibit
   parts of the museum

4. *X is a reason for Y*
   reasons for getting mad
   reasons to move on to next exhibit
   reasons to be bored
   reasons for being at the museum

5. *X is a stage in Y*
   stages in moving through the area
   stages in looking at each exhibit

6. *X is used for Y*
   things to do with your hands
   things to do with your feet

Although this list is incomplete, it gives a general idea about possible areas for further research. It is a beginning overview of the social situation common in museums. In most published ethnographic studies, the author does not provide a complete list of cultural domains. Rather, most ethnographers select from the larger list to focus on several related domains in the final description. For example, in his study of flea markets, Maisel (1974) discusses a limited number of domains including (1) kinds of goods, (2) reasons people go to flea markets, (3) kinds of flea market action, and (4) kinds of myths. In the following steps we will discuss how to select domains for more intensive study, but any selection is premature if you have not first developed a detailed list of cultural domains.

In this step we have examined the nature of ethnographic analysis and the procedures for discovering cultural domains. A cultural domain is an important unit that exists in every culture. It is a category of cultural meaning that includes other smaller categories. Domain analysis, when doing participant observation, includes six interrelated steps:

1. Selecting a single semantic relationship.

2. Preparing a domain analysis worksheet.
3. Selecting a sample of fieldnote entries.
4. Searching for possible cover terms and included terms that appropriately fit the semantic relationship.
5. Repeating the search with other semantic relationships.
6. Making a list of all identified domains.

Domain analysis is not a once-and-for-all procedure. It must be repeated as new data are collected through participant observation. Every few weeks throughout a research project, the ethnographer will want to use these procedures to find new domains.

Tasks

5.1 Conduct a thorough domain analysis following the steps presented in this step. Base your analysis on all your expanded fieldnotes collected to date.

5.2 Make a summary list of all domains identified through your analysis and review it to ascertain possible domains for further research.

5.3 Conduct a period of participant observation in which you make additional descriptive observations.

OBJECTIVES
1. To select a tentative focus for participant observation.
2. To learn how structural questions lead to focused observations.
3. To learn to make focused observations.
4. To conduct a period of participant observation in which you add focused observations to your activities.

Let us review briefly where the Developmental Research Sequence has brought us. We began with three preparatory steps: (1) Selecting a Social Situation; (2) Doing Participant Observation; and, (3) Making an Ethnographic Record. With Step Three you had made a selection and actually started your fieldwork. Step Four examined strategies for (4) Making Descriptive Observations. Using the fieldnotes you had collected, we went on to begin ethnographic analysis by (5) Making a Domain Analysis, which resulted in a broad overview of the cultural scene with a long list of cultural domains. After making another trip to the field and taking more fieldnotes, you will probably be able to add to this list.

Depending on the amount of time spent doing participant observation and making your analysis, you have probably become keenly aware of what I shall call *cultural complexity,* the fact that even the simplest social situation is imbued with a large number of cultural meanings. Take, for example, a flea market. Vendors come to the market early in the morning, set up their stalls and tables, display their goods, and then wait for customers. The flea market lasts for five or six hours, then people leave. On the surface it looks like a simple social situation. But, as Maisel (1974) discovered, the phenomenon of a flea market is *culturally complex.* After interviews with more than seventy persons, many hours of observations, and after five years of participating in flea markets, he had not come to a complete understanding of this cultural scene. In his ethnographic report, Maisel chose to emphasize data related to "the action" that occurs at flea markets.

Like all ethnographers, you will discover that cultural complexity makes it difficult to describe a cultural scene in a completely thorough manner. An exhaustive ethnography, even for a rather limited cultural scene, would take years of intensive research. All ethnographers, whether studying the total way of life in an Eskimo community or a Bushmen band, or investigating a limited cultural scene in a large city, must limit their investigation in some way. Some aspects of the culture will have to be studied more exhaustively than others. In this step I want to discuss how to limit the scope of your ethnography while maintaining a holistic viewpoint.

SELECTING AN ETHNOGRAPHIC FOCUS

When Maisel (1974) decided to study "the action" at flea markets, he selected an ethnographic focus. A focus refers to a single cultural domain or a few related domains and the relationships of such domains to the rest of the cultural scene. At first it is difficult to know which domains will cluster together in such a way as to provide an ethnographic focus. You will have to make your selection *tentative*, beginning with a single cultural domain or several that appear to be related. As your research progresses over the next few periods of investigation, you may discard or refine this original focus.

Whether to select an ethnographic focus or not is a decision each investigator must make. You can either carry out a *surface investigation*, identifying and partially studying as many cultural domains as possible, or you can select an ethnographic focus and conduct an *in-depth investigation*. If you decide on this second strategy, you will obviously have to neglect many important features of the cultural scene. After spending many months making a surface investigation, some investigators will then focus their research after making one or two preliminary reports. Others will decide ahead of time on a specific problem for study, making the choice for an in-depth investigation before the first trip to the field. For example, Walum (1974) decided beforehand that her ethnographic focus in observing people going through doors on a college campus would be on male-female relationships. This same project could have been done with an alternative ethnographic focus such as the ways people communicate nonverbally when going through doors.

Ethnographers have long debated the advantages of in-depth and surface strategies. Those who advocate the in-depth strategy argue that cultural meaning is complex and if we only skim the surface we will never know how informants really understand things. It is better, they say, to study a single domain intensively than many domains superficially.

Those who advocate studying the surface of cultural meanings argue that we need to see a culture or cultural scene in holistic terms. It is the relationships among domains that are important; then later, if time allows, we can come back and examine each domain in exhaustive detail.

In actual practice, most ethnographers adopt a compromise. They study a few selected domains (an ethnographic focus) in-depth, while still attempting to gain a surface understanding of the cultural scene as a whole. In order to accomplish this, we must adopt strategies for both in-depth analysis and a more holistic, surface analysis. The steps in the D.R.S. Method are designed to keep a balanced tension between these two strategies. In the first five steps you were going in the direction of a broad, surface investigation. In the next four steps (including this one) you will shift to learning the skills needed to make an in-depth investigation. Then, in the last three steps we will again shift back to a broader perspective, trying to see how the ethnographic focus you select is related to the rest of the cultural scene. Those who have limited time or different goals may use this book effectively and go immediately to Step Ten: Making a Theme Analysis. These two different emphases throughout the twelve steps of the D.R.S. Method are shown in Figure 12.

General Cultural Domains

Before you can make a valid selection for your ethnographic focus, you must first identify a wide range of possibilities. All ethnographic problem solving begins by identifying the *problem* ("I must narrow my investigation"), identifying the *cause* ("Culture is complex"), and then listing a large number of *possible solutions* ("a long list of cultural domains"). If you have only identified ten or fifteen domains in your cultural scene, you are not ready to select a focus. You must go back to your fieldnotes or make more observations to identify many more cultural domains.

One aid in expanding your list of cultural domains comes from considering what I call certain "general cultural domains," categories of cultural meaning that occur in almost every social situation. They are stated in such general terms that they can help you think of *specific* domains to look for in your fieldnotes. Each domain is still stated with a cover term and semantic relationship; the included terms must be discovered from your particular cultural scene. Many of these general cultural domains are based on the nine dimensions of social situations presented earlier: *space, object, act, activity, event, time, actor, goal, feeling.* I will list some general domains but you will undoubtedly be able to think of more.

1. *Strict inclusion: X is a kind of Y*
   kinds of acts
   kinds of places
   kinds of objects
   kinds of activities
   kinds of relationships

   kinds of time
   kinds of actors
   kinds of feelings
   kinds of goals

2. *Spatial: X is a part of Y*
   parts of activities
   parts of places
   parts of events
   parts of objects

FIGURE 12. Focus in Ethnographic Research

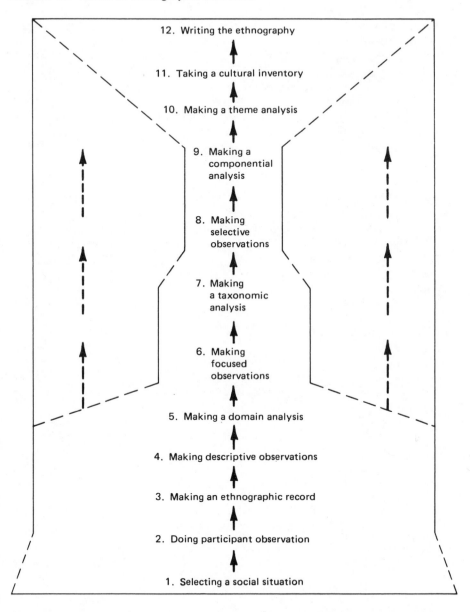

12. Writing the ethnography

11. Taking a cultural inventory

10. Making a theme analysis

9. Making a componential analysis

8. Making selective observations

7. Making a taxonomic analysis

6. Making focused observations

5. Making a domain analysis

4. Making descriptive observations

3. Making an ethnographic record

2. Doing participant observation

1. Selecting a social situation

The D.R.S. steps begin with a wide focus, surveying many possible social situations. When one is selected, the research includes the *entire* social situation from Steps 3 through 12. However, there is a dual focus, one narrow, the other broad and holistic. The ethnographer continues to use the skills learned in Steps 4 and 5 while at the same time focusing observations on selected cultural domains. Toward the end of the project the focus expands again to make a holistic description of the cultural scene.

3. *Cause-effect: X is a result of Y*
   results of activities
   results of acts
   results of events
   results of feelings

4. *Rationale: X is a reason for doing Y*
   reasons for actions
   reasons for carrying out activities
   reasons for staging events
   reasons for feelings
   reasons for using objects
   reasons for seeking goals
   reasons for arranging space

5. *Location for action: X is a place for doing Y*
   places for activities
   places where people act
   places where events are held
   places for objects
   places for seeking goals

6. *Function: X is used for Y*
   uses for objects
   uses for events
   uses for acts
   uses for activities
   uses for feelings
   uses for places

7. *Means-end: X is a way to do Y*
   ways to organize space
   ways to act
   ways to carry out activities
   ways to stage events
   ways to seek goals
   ways to become actors
   ways to feel

8. *Sequence: X is a step in Y*
   steps in achieving goals
   steps in an act
   stages in an event
   stages in an activity
   stages in becoming an actor

9. *Attribution: X is an attribute of Y* (characteristic)
   characteristics of objects
   characteristics of places
   characteristics of time
   characteristics of actors
   characteristics of activities

In making use of these general cultural domains, you will have to replace the general cover terms such as "object" and "actor" with specific types, each of which will have many included terms. For example, in my study of the grand jury, I used the general domain "kinds of actors" as a guide to focusing my attention on domains of this sort. Rather than identifying all the people involved in the grand jury under this domain, I identified several domains. These included (1) kinds of witnesses, (2) kinds of grand jurors, and (3) kinds of officials. The general domain thus led me to three culturally specific domains. Once you have used these general domains to enlarge your list of cultural domains, you are ready to consider selecting a focus.

Criteria for Selecting an Ethnographic Focus

1. Personal Interest.   If you are a beginning ethnographer and your goal is primarily to learn to do participant observation, almost any domain or cluster of domains can become your focus. Look over the domains you have identified and ask yourself, "Which ones look most interesting?" Perhaps you have done previous research or read an article that will suggest something of interest. If you select a domain for more intensive study and discover it offers few possibilities, you can discard it and move on to another you find interesting.

2. Suggestions by Informants.   Sometimes the people you are observing will make suggestions about things they feel are important. You can then take their advice as the basis for selecting an ethnographic focus. In our study of a college bar (Spradley and Mann 1975), one of the waitresses suggested, "If you really want to understand Brady's Bar, you should study the problems waitresses have with bartenders." This led to a research focus on domains like "kinds of bartenders," "ways bartenders hassle waitresses," and "ways to get along with bartenders." If you listen to what people say, they often drop hints as to what they feel is important in their worlds. A man standing in line at a bank may mutter, "Every time I change to a faster line, it slows up and I have to wait longer." This might give you a clue that studying domains like "ways to choose a line" and "reasons for changing lines" might be interesting. Sometimes an informant will refer to something so often that it stands out as important. For example, the prosecuting attorney on the grand jury would constantly remind the jurors that "we have lots of cases, we must hurry today." This emphasis on speeding up the process led me to several domains including "ways the attorney speeds things up," "ways to keep jurors from asking questions," "ways to hurry witnesses," and "things that slow down the process." If you develop a close relationship with anyone in the social situation you are studying you might ask them, "What do you feel is most important for me to find out about?"

3. Theoretical Interest.   Some cultural domains relate well to social science theories. Let's say, for example, that you are interested in some theory of social organization as it applies to schools. You begin observing in a third-grade class and identify many domains. Several of these will be specifically related to social organization, including such things as "kinds of kids," "kinds of teachers," and "kinds of groups." If you are interested in the way people manage privacy in public places, you could focus on domains such as "kinds of intrusions," "ways to avoid people," and "ways to appear inconspicuous." You may have selected a particular social situation on the basis of some theoretical interest. Now, as you look for an ethnographic focus you can use that interest to narrow your research.

4. Strategic Ethnography.   In an earlier chapter I discussed ways in which ethnography can be carried out in the service of human needs. I listed several major problem areas in our own culture and suggested these could help guide the ethnographer in selecting a cultural scene for research. These same criteria can guide you now in selecting a focus for research in a particular cultural scene. For example, I began studying a city jail (Spradley 1970) because of reports from informants that it was degrading and actually violated the rights of prisoners. Once into the study I selected "kinds of inmates," and "parts of the bucket" to explore more fully what the prisoners experienced throughout the jail. Some domains in a culture offer special opportunities to carry out strategic ethnography.

5. Organizing Domains.   Sometimes you will discover a large domain that seems to organize most of the cultural meaning of a particular scene. Somehow, it pulls together the relationships among many other domains. For example, after many months of listening to tramps talk about life in the Seattle City Jail (the bucket), I saw that one domain seemed to tie all the information together. I called it "stages in making the bucket" and it became an important ethnographic focus.

I have found from experience and reviewing the work of hundreds of ethnographers that domains based on *sequence relationships* frequently help to organize a cultural scene. Let's say you are observing shoppers in a supermarket. As you watch them come in the door, you take a basket and follow them throughout the store and observe them leaving. Now, there are hundreds of domains in this cultural scene—kinds of food, ways to select, patterns of movement, places in the store, and ways customers interact to name but a few. You could, however, show the cultural scene in a holistic manner by focusing on "stages in shopping." This domain would identify stages like the following:

Stage 1: entering the store
Stage 2: selecting a shopping cart
Stage 3: choosing a direction or route
Stage 4: picking out meat
Stage 5: getting dairy products
Stage 6: buying produce
Stage 7: selecting a check-out line
Stage 8: checking out
Stage 9: transporting groceries
Stage 10: leaving the store

Within this large organizing domain, you might still want to focus your research even more specifically. For example, you might find that most of the interaction between customers and employees occurs at the check-out stand. You might want to focus on two related cultural domains "kinds of customer-employee relationships" and "kinds of check-out conflicts." Selecting an organizing domain for your ethnographic focus can be of enormous help when you finally reach the point of writing your ethnography. The domain can become the major subpoints in your paper.

FOCUSED OBSERVATIONS

Once you have selected an ethnographic focus you are ready to go back to your social situation and add focused observations to your repertoire of fieldwork activities. Although focused observations will increasingly take up a major part of your time, they will never occupy all the time spent during a period of participant observation. Figure 13 shows the relationship of observation time over the course of your research to the three kinds of observation.

Focused observations are based on the second type of ethnographic question, one I call a *structural question*. A structural question makes use of the semantic relationship of a domain with the cover term. Listed below are several domains I have used in previous examples along with the appropriate structural question:

DOMAIN	STRUCTURAL QUESTION
stages in shopping	What are all the stages in shopping?
kinds of witnesses	What are all the kinds of witnesses?

reasons for changing lines	What are all the reasons people change lines?
ways to hurry witnesses	What are all the ways to hurry witnesses?
parts of the bucket	What are all the parts of the bucket?
causes of conflict	What are all the causes of conflict?

Let's take a specific example of how one might use structural questions in research. Sugarman spent two months in the summer of 1968 as a full-time

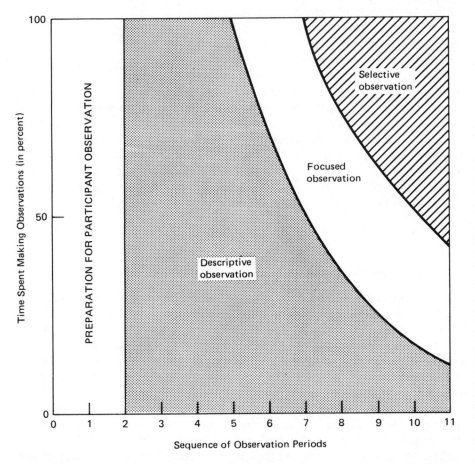

The amount of time spent making observations during your research project can be divided in terms of the kind of observation. The first two periods in the D.R.S. process are spent preparing for research. Then begin three periods of *descriptive observation*. Beginning with this step you will phase in *focused observation*, slackening but not eliminating descriptive ones. The seventh period will usher in *selective observation*. All continue at the same time.

FIGURE 13. The Relationship of Observation Time to the Three Kinds of Observation

participant observer in a drug rehabilitation center. In his ethnography *Daytop Village: A Therapeutic Community* (1974), he describes many domains in the culture of this community. One domain he focused on was called "kinds of social roles" in the encounter group. Once having identified this as a domain, he could carry out focused observation with the structural question in mind: "What are all the social roles people play in the encounter group?" By asking this question over and over again during encounter-group sessions, he discovered the following *included terms* that made up this domain. The result was an analytic domain, one made up of terms created by the investigator to describe the cultural rules for behavior in the encounter group. Here are the roles Sugarman identified:

1. chairman
2. prosecutor
3. witness
4. identifier
5. preacher

6. reflector
7. irritant
8. therapist
9. patch-up artist

The major feature of structural questions is that they are *repeatable*. You will need to ask them over and over again. One of the best ways to avoid shallow ethnographic research is to formulate structural questions carefully, then make focused observations that are based entirely on a single structural question. Sugarman, for example, could sit through many hours of encounter group at Daytop Village asking, "Are there any other roles these group members are playing?" Each new role observed is another answer to the structural question.

Consider the way structural questions can lead to focused observations in another setting. Tolzmann (1978) set out to study interaction among strangers in an urban arcade. The arcade was indoors, and it had benches on which people could sit. Several passageways led away from the arcade: one to a large hotel, another to a parking ramp, and another to a downtown street. Many people walked through the arcade to the parking ramp, but others sat on the benches, wandered through the small stores that opened on the arcade, or simply loitered in this general area. At first, through descriptive observations Tolzmann described this general pattern of activity, trying to find some specific areas for an ethnographic focus. Through domain analysis she identified at least the following domains:

1. uses of the arcade
2. kinds of danger signals in the arcade
3. ways to manage danger
4. kinds of people in the arcade

With these domains in mind she formulated structural questions and returned to the arcade to make focused observations. "What are all the uses of the arcade?" led to discovering the following cultural patterns: *shop, wait, get from outside, use restroom, eat, talk, use telephone, walk through,* and *hustle.* A number of people, including elderly women, used the arcade as a place to go, a kind of "home away from home." These "regulars" recognized that the arcade held certain dangers, and knowing the danger signals was one way they could cope with the dangers of this impersonal urban place. One evidence that dangers existed was the fact that a uniformed guard patrolled the passageways and the arcade itself. "What are all the danger signals in the arcade?" became an important structural question Tolzmann used to make focused observations. Instead of trying to watch everything that went on in the arcade, she was able to focus on things that were clear danger signals to the arcade's regular inhabitants. This domain included such things as *crowdedness, emptiness, absence of the guard, people sitting too close, people talking too loud,* and *those times when all shops closed.*

It is possible to make focused observations on several domains at the same time. Tolzmann, for example, could watch for danger signals, ways people manage danger, and the uses of the arcade all at the same time. It is a good idea to prepare five or six structural questions before going on to make focused observations. With these in mind, you can take up an observation post and look for the answers to your questions. Remember, your goal is not to find a single answer to a question, such as a single danger signal or way to deal with danger. Rather, you want to ask the question over and over and find as many answers as you can.

Let's take one more example of making focused observations. Walum (1974), in her study of male-female encounters at doors on a college campus, discovered numerous cultural domains. At one time in the past it was widely accepted that males could show their courtesy by opening doors for females. With changing definitions of equality, this door ceremony has begun to change. But, as Walum discovered, the change has not occurred uniformly among college students and different patterns emerged from her observations. She created an analytic domain, "kinds of door openers," and began to make focused observations to discover the patterns that existed. "What are all the different kinds of door openers?" She discovered the following:

1. *The confused.* In this situation, neither male nor female knows what to do and often stop and bump into each other.
2. *The tester.* This person opens the door for females, but asks questions like, "Are you a liberated woman?" Or a woman will ask, "Aren't you going to open the door?"
3. *The humanitarian.* This person will try to be sensitive to the needs of the situation, offering to open the door or letting the other open it.
4. *The defender.* This person defends the status quo. If female, she waits

until a male opens the door. If, male, he rushes forward to open it and prevent a female from usurping his right.

5. *The rebel.* This person does exactly the opposite of the defender. This pattern is represented by males who refuse to open doors and women who refuse to allow males to open doors.

Here are four simple suggestions that may help you plan for making focused observations:

1. List the domains you have tentatively selected for focused observations.
2. Write out the structural questions to ask yourself as you observe.
3. Identify observation posts that would give you the best opportunity to make your focused observations.
4. Identify activities in which you might participate to carry out your focused observations.

In this step we have examined ways to select an ethnographic focus and then how to carry out observations to study this smaller area of social behavior. In addition to narrowing the scope of your research, you will be able to discover the structure of a particular cultural scene. Every scene is made up of numerous cultural domains, and every domain has many smaller categories included in them. Focused observation leads to discovering both the larger and smaller categories that make up a cultural scene.

Tasks

6.1 Enlarge your list of cultural domains by making use of the general cultural domains presented in this step.

6.2 Using this list, select a tentative ethnographic focus of one or more cultural domains.

6.3 Conduct a focused observation in the field after you have made careful plans for that observation.

MAKING A TAXONOMIC ANALYSIS

1. To understand how taxonomies organize cultural domains.
2. To learn how to make a taxonomic analysis.
3. To construct a taxonomy for one or more domains by following the steps for doing taxonomic analysis.

The ethnographer begins an in-depth investigation by selecting several cultural domains for careful study. The first goal is to discover as many members of a domain as possible. It means finding out as many different *kinds of witnesses* as appear before the grand jury or discovering as many *stages in shopping* as possible. Through carefully focused observations the ethnographer learns to make explicit those distinctions people are making in everyday life.

In this step we want to go even deeper in our investigation of cultural domains by finding out how they are organized. At first a domain looks like a large box filled with smaller categories of behavior. On closer examination, though, you will discover that many times the contents of this "box" are systematically organized. You may even discover that the domain you have examined is part of a much larger domain. Cultural meaning arises, in part, from the way things are organized, the way they are related to one another. This organization can be represented by means of a taxonomy.

TAXONOMY

Like a cultural domain, a taxonomy is a set of categories organized on the basis of a single semantic relationship. The major difference between the two is that a taxonomy shows more of the relationships among the things inside the cultural domain. Let's take a simple example. I stop at a drugstore to buy a magazine, and without thinking I make use of the cultural domain "kinds of magazines." Looking across the rack I see *Saturday Review, Harpers, Popular Mechanics, T.V. Guide, Superman Comics, Batman,* and *Cosmopolitan.* I'm not interested in comics; I don't want a woman's magazine so I skip over *Better Homes and Gardens.* I want to buy *Time,* a newsmagazine. Then I spot *U.S. News and World Report* and know that I'm close. There, hidden from view behind *Newsweek* is the last copy of *Time*. I pick it up, take it to the check-out counter, and pay for it before leaving the store. Now, all these magazines are members of the domain "kinds of magazines," but within that domain I have other sub-categories for organizing it in more detail. We can show this difference in the following diagram:

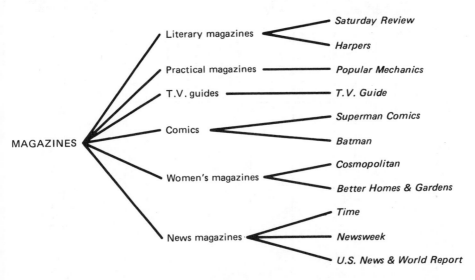

A taxonomy, then, differs from a domain in only one respect: it shows the relationships among *all* the included terms in a domain. A taxonomy reveals subsets and the way they are related to the whole.

Consider another example of a taxonomy, this time from an ethnography of tuna fishermen who work out of San Diego, California. Orbach, an anthropologist, describes the culture of this group in his book *Hunters, Seamen, and Entrepreneurs* (1977). One of the first things he had to learn through participant observation was the cultural meaning of the ship used for fishing. Orbach identifies a large cultural domain that includes nearly thirty different spaces or *parts of a tunaboat* identified as follows:

the stack	netpile	main deckhouse
skipper's cabin	anchor winches	main working deck
seine net	rail-mounted winch	bridge
skiff	below	crow's nest
main winch	on deck	shaft alley
deck hatch	up top	main engine room
shark slide	platform	mast
brailing booms	well deck	speedboat deck
cabins	upper engine room	deck
galley	the bow	

FIGURE 14. Taxonomy of Parts of a Tunaboat

PARTS OF A TUNABOAT				
SHAFT ALLEY				
MAIN ENGINE ROOM				
MAST	Crow's nest			
	Platform			
DECK	UP TOP (upper deck)	Speedboat deck		
		Bridge	The stack	
			Skipper's cabin	
	ON DECK (middle deck)	Netpile	Seine net	
			Skiff	
		Main working deck	Main winch	
			Deck hatch	
			Shark slide	
			Brailing booms	
	BELOW (lower deck)	Main deckhouse	Cabins	
			Galley	
		The bow	Anchor winches	
			Rail-mounted winch	
		Well deck		
		Upper engine room		

114

All these terms are included in the domain by a single semantic relationship: X is a part of Y. Each term represents a part of the tunaboat. However, this listing does not show us that the *anchor winch* is part of the *bow,* or any of the other internal relationships of the domain. From Orbach's description it is possible to identify many such relationships and construct a taxonomy to show how the domain is organized (Figure 14). Although not exhaustive, this taxonomy does show that numerous relationships occur within the domain.

This taxonomy reveals an important feature of all taxonomies: they have different *levels.* At a minimum, with a cover term and included terms, a taxonomy has two levels as in this example:

KINDS OF OBSERVATION		
Descriptive observation	Focused observation	Selective observation

The taxonomy "parts of a tunaboat" has five different levels, from the top to the most specific terms at the bottom.

Like domains, taxonomies can be constructed from folk terms, analytic terms, or a mixture of each. In Sugarman's study of a drug rehabilitation community, he observed many different activities intended to punish or reward members and lumped these together into a cultural domain called "kinds of sanctions." This was not a folk term and neither were the two major subcategories in the taxonomy: positive sanctions and negative sanctions. However, most of the other terms were ones used by informants. They are shown in the following mixed taxonomy (Sugarman 1974).

Sanctions

1. Positive Sanctions
    1.1. getting privileges
        1.11. possession of clothing
        1.12. possession of personal item
        1.13. permission to grow sideburns
        1.14. permission to go out
        1.15. permission to read
    1.2 getting promotion
2. Negative Sanctions
    2.1. getting a pull-up
    2.2. getting a haircut
    2.3. having to wear a sign
    2.4. carrying a symbol
    2.5. getting your head shaved

TAXONOMIC ANALYSIS

In Step Five, we defined ethnographic analysis as a *search for the parts of a culture, the relationships among the parts, and their relationships to the whole*. From the cultural scene as a whole we moved to identifying basic parts of a culture (domains) and the smaller units that make up these domains (cover terms and included terms). Now we are ready to search for the relationships among these smaller units, the included terms in the domain. Later we will examine these relationships in even greater detail through componential analysis. Then we will be ready to move back to studying the relationship of domains to the whole culture or cultural scene.

The experienced ethnographer often combines domain analysis and taxonomic analysis into a single process because the latter is an extension of domain analysis. But, in order to do them, it is best to treat them separately. By following the procedures outlined below you will find it possible to make a rigorous analysis of any domain in a cultural scene.

Step One: Select a domain for taxonomic analysis. Begin with a domain for which you have the most information. You will undoubtedly discover additional included terms as you make your analysis, but the more you have to begin with, the easier the analysis. For purposes of illustration, let's take the ten stages presented earlier for shopping in a supermarket:

Stage 1: entering the store
Stage 2: selecting a shopping cart
Stage 3: choosing a direction or route
Stage 4: picking out meat
Stage 5: getting dairy products
Stage 6: buying produce
Stage 7: selecting a check-out line
Stage 8: checking out
Stage 9: transporting groceries
Stage 10: leaving the store

This list represents a preliminary one that taxonomic analysis will help to expand and revise.

Step Two: Look for similarities based on the same semantic relationship. At this point in the example, we have identified only a single set of terms that are at the same level in the taxonomy. Now we want to know if we can usefully divide these terms into two or more subsets. Looking for similarities is best done with a question that asks: "Are any of these similar because they can go together as a single larger stage?" Looking over the above list, it is easy to see that Stages 4, 5, and 6 might be considered similar, since they are all steps in "selecting groceries." In fact, once this similarity is recognized, it helps to resolve a problem. Although most people follow the order of picking out meat, then dairy products, then produce, not everyone follows it. Some people actually go through the store in the opposite direction. The order of the ten stages represented what most people do. It also leaves out many smaller items such as the bakery or health foods. It now begins to look like grouping these three into a single stage would fit the observations better:

Stage 4: Selecting Groceries
   Stage 4.1: picking out meat
   Stage 4.2: getting dairy products
   Stage 4.3: buying frozen goods
   Stage 4.4: selecting health foods
   Stage 4.5: buying produce

You can now go back to the supermarket and begin watching to see. if there are any other stages in this larger subcategory of selecting groceries. Although you have identified five substages, you will need to make a note in your final ethnography that people do not always follow that order.

As you look over the original list of stages, you recall hearing someone say to a friend, "I'm going to check out now." They were some distance from the long lines at the check-out counters and you watched them select a line, wait in line, and then go through the process of checking out. You now think it would match your observations better to put Stage 7, selecting a check-out line, and Stage 8, checking out, together into a single stage. Once you make that decision, other things come to mind and you now create a new Stage 5 that looks like this:

Stage 5: Checking Out
   Stage 5.1: selecting a line
   Stage 5.2: waiting in line
   Stage 5.3: unloading the cart
   Stage 5.4: paying the bill
   Stage 5.5: leaving the check-out counter

By looking for similarities you will do more than regroup members of a domain. Often it leads to discovering more cultural categories and new insights into the cultural scene you are studying.

Step Three: Look for additional included terms. You will recall that you discovered the included terms in a domain by asking a structural question using the *cover term.* So, for example, for the domain *kinds of witnesses* one merely asks, "What are all the different kinds of witnesses?" Or, in studying "stages in shopping" at a supermarket, one asks, "What are all the stages in shopping?"

Now, in order to discover additional included terms you will need to apply a structural question *to each included term.* Take the stages in shopping, as revised, and note the numerous structural questions we can ask. "Are there different stages of entering the store?" "Are there different stages in selecting a shopping cart?" "Are there different stages in checking out?" "Are there different stages in paying the bill?" It should be clear that each question will receive an affirmative answer, and you could easily supply many of the answers.

Let's look at another example. In Hanson's study (1978) of parents and children in a museum mentioned earlier, it was relatively easy to identify "the teacher" as one kind of parent. This type of person, whether mother or father, was constantly instructing the children as they moved from one display to another. It was clear that the teacher was a kind of parent. But the structural question for the domain ("What are all the kinds of parents?") could also be used for this particular type ("What are all the kinds of teachers?"). Using this question in focused observations, Hanson discovered the following types of teachers:

Kinds of Parents

1. The Teacher
   1.1 the knowledge sharer
   1.2 the lecturer
   1.3 the tutor
   1.4 the question-answerer
   1.5 the discussion leader
2. etc.

You will find that using structural questions in this way is one of the most powerful devices for expanding your observations of ethnographic detail. It will keep you from overlooking much important information.

Step Four: Search for larger, more inclusive domains that might include as a subset the domain you are analyzing. Imagine that you set out to study the lives of patients in a large state mental hospital as Goffman did (1961). As a participant observer you spend a great deal of time with patients, informally taking part in what goes on. After a few weeks you notice that many patients collect things from wastebaskets and garbage boxes. Some patients acquire numerous possessions in this manner, a practice frowned upon by the staff but seldom forbidden. You identify a cultural domain called "kinds of scavenging," which has at least the following included terms:

1. searching through refuse dumps
2. looking for newspapers in wastebaskets

3. examining wooden storage boxes
4. searching ashtrays for usable butts

Now you begin to make a taxonomic analysis and search for some larger domain that might include scavenging as a subset. It strikes you that there are numerous illegitimate ways to get what one desires, ways to get around the structure of rules in the institution, so you formulate a cover term for a larger domain: "working the system." This domain includes *scavenging, food-getting, social association with outsiders, obtaining a workable assignment,* and even *hospitalization* itself. Like scavenging, each of these categories has subcategories included in them, but you still can ask whether "working the system" is part of a larger domain. Goffman (1961) identified a larger analytic domain which he called "secondary adjustments," the things patients did to get by in a hospital. He had two general categories: *using make-dos* and *working the system.*

One can begin to search for larger, more inclusive domains by asking a structural question in reverse: "Is this domain (kinds of trees) a kind of something else?" or "Is this domain (stages in shopping) a stage in something else?" Reviewing the "general domains" presented in the last chapter can give some clues to larger, more inclusive domains.

Step Five: Construct a tentative taxonomy.   A taxonomy can be represented in several ways: a box diagram, a set of lines and nodes, or an outline. Figure 15 shows these three methods of representation.

Step Six: Make focused observations to check out your analysis.   Any taxonomic analysis will lead to new observations in the field. Let's say you are studying the stages in shopping in a supermarket. Now that you have grouped several activities under *"Stage 5: Checking Out,"* you need to go back and look at the entire sequence of checking out more carefully. Are there any subparts you missed? You have also asked structural questions about each of the stages which can lead to new observations. For instance, the first stage was "entering the store." When you asked yourself, "Are there different stages in entering a supermarket?" you realized you had overlooked this entire area of activity. You assumed that people simply *entered the store,* but now you're not so sure. During your next visit to the store you discover that entering can be divided into five stages, each quite complex and each part of the overall cultural pattern. Your taxonomic analysis thus leads back to making more focused observations.

Step Seven: Construct a completed taxonomy.   At some point it becomes necessary to stop collecting more data and stop analyzing a taxonomy, accepting it as relatively complete. It is well to recognize that taxonomies always approximate the cultural patterns you have observed. There will be

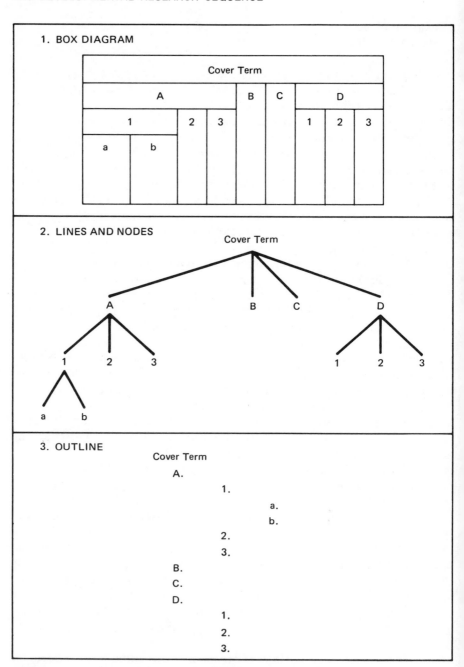

FIGURE 15. Types of Taxonomic Diagrams

exceptions which you will have to note in your final ethnographic description. Even when you have worked out a complete folk taxonomy, one elicited from informants, it will only approximate the cultural knowledge of these informants. More important, you can go on to make selected observations and make a componential analysis even though your taxonomy is incomplete in some way. As stated earlier, ethnography is both science and art. We seek to discover the cultural patterns people use to make sense out of their worlds. At the same time we recognize that every ethnographer solves problems in ways that go beyond the data or on the basis of insufficient data. Construct a taxonomy to represent each domain you have analyzed, and go on to the next research strategies.

Tasks

7.1 Conduct a taxonomic analysis on one or more domains, following the steps presented in this chapter.

7.2 Carry out a period of participant observation using both descriptive observations and focused observations. Use your focused observations to check out your taxonomic analysis.

7.3 Prepare a completed taxonomic diagram of one or more domains.

MAKING SELECTED OBSERVATIONS

OBJECTIVES
1. To learn how ethnographic interviews can be used in participant observation.
2. To understand how contrast questions lead to selected observations.
3. To learn to make selected observations.

In the last few steps we have moved from the broad surface of many domains in a cultural scene to an in-depth analysis of a few domains in an *ethnographic focus.* By now you should have completed a taxonomic analysis of at least one domain. You probably have several other taxonomies in various stages of development. In addition to making focused observations, you have continued to make descriptive observations which have undoubtedly led to a longer list of cultural domains. You may have shifted from a tentative ethnographic focus to a different one that is more strategic for understanding the cultural scene. Such changes in direction are common in ethnographic research and should not cause the ethnographer to regret earlier choices. One of the challenging features of doing ethnography is that one cannot tell where it will lead ahead of time. New discoveries open new doors to cultural understanding.

One of the changes that occurs after five or six periods of field observation in most scenes is that you become recognized by people in the social situation. You may have had the opportunity to explain your project; several people may have observed you taking notes and inquired about your work. It may only be that you are on a smile-and-nod recognition basis with people, but you are no longer a complete stranger. This fact offers opportunities for conducting ethnographic interviews during participant observation. Although the primary emphasis of this book is on *observation techniques,* some readers may find they cannot pass up the valuable chance to interview one or more informants. Another book, *The Ethnographic Interview* (Spradley 1979), examines the entire ethnographic research cycle from the perspective of interviewing. At this point I only want to suggest ways that will enable you to capitalize on interviewing opportunities that present themselves during participant observation.

INTERVIEWS AND PARTICIPANT OBSERVATION

There are many different forms of interviewing. Ethnographic interviewing is a special kind that employs questions designed to discover the cultural meanings people have learned. Such interviews make use of descriptive questions (discussed in Step Four), structural questions (discussed in Step Six), and contrast questions (discussed in Step Eight). Participant observers formulate specific ethnographic questions and then *ask themselves* these questions. They come up with answers from fieldnotes or new observations. Or, in many cases, after several periods of field investigation you may answer your own ethnographic questions out of your own memory. In a real sense, you are treating yourself as an informant for a particular cultural scene.

If you decide to conduct ethnographic interviews, you can simply make use of the same questions with one or more informants. It is useful to distinguish between two types of interviews: informal and formal.

Informal Ethnographic Interviews

An informal ethnographic interview occurs whenever you ask someone a question during the course of participant observation. In my research on the grand jury I found many opportunities for informal interviews. For example, I wanted to know all the "kinds of cases" that were brought before the grand jury. I made observations, writing down each type as the weeks went by, but I knew there were others and so I merely asked the prosecuting attorney, "What other kinds of cases come before the grand jury?" In fact, there were many opportunities to ask questions as a member of the grand jury, and I simply asked ethnographic questions. About the third month it was announced that one of the duties of the grand jury was to inspect the jails in Marshall County. It was presented as an optional activity; a few people might want to visit nearby jails. At this point it was possible during the group meeting to raise my hand and ask, "What are all the different jails in Marshall County?" I had identified a cultural domain and conducted an informal interview. In addition, each coffee break that occurred offered chances to talk to other jurors. On more than one occasion I would engage people in conversations and then ask some ethnographic question that was appropriate to the conversation.

Consider the hypothetical case introduced earlier of studying a supermarket. As a participant observer you would have many opportunities to ask ethnographic questions informally. You could pick up a few items for purchase and then get in a long line to wait. Striking up a conversation with the next person in line, you might say, "It sure is difficult to find the line that moves the fastest." This opener could lead to questions about the domain "ways to select a line." "How do you decide to select a line?" or "What kinds of things make a line move fast?'' Customers often talk to the check-out person and you could hold informal interviews each time you go through the line. For example, you might discover that these employees treated customers differently. You formulate a tentative domain ''kinds of custom-ers'' at the check-out counter, from observation identifying *check writers, food-stamp people, regulars,* and *children.* After you become recognized by one or more check-out people, you could ask casually as you pay your bill, ''You sure have a lot of different people come through here. Are there different kinds of customers?'' If you have informed the person of your research project, it might be relatively easy to pick a slow time, purchase a few groceries, and then stand and talk, asking several informal ethnographic questions.

Formal Ethnographic Interviews

A formal interview usually occurs at an appointed time and results from a specific request to hold the interview. If you have developed friendly rela-tionships with people in the social situation, you may want to ask for such interviews. ''I'd like to get your ideas about what goes on in the supermar-ket'' might be sufficient for going on to set up an interview. Don't overlook informants who are previous acquaintances. For example, if you are study-ing a supermarket near your campus, there are undoubtedly some students who have frequented the store. Ask your friends if they ever shop there, and when you find one, ask for an interview. Or, if you are studying the cultural rules for riding the bus, ask your friends if they ride the bus often, and when you find one, ask for an interview.

It is probably best to begin formal interviews with descriptive questions. ''Can you describe to me what you do when you shop at the supermarket, from the time you enter the store until you leave?'' This question could easily add new categories or clarify relationships in your domain, ''stages in shopping.'' In the same interview you could ask other descriptive questions as well as both structural questions and contrast questions to be discussed later in this step. It is a good idea to tape record each interview as well as taking copious notes. From such an interview you may find folk terms you will want to use to replace analytic terms in one or more taxonomies.

All informants are participant observers without knowing it. When you ask them ethnographic questions you tap their knowledge about a particular cultural scene; you are making use of their informal skills as participant observers. Your own observations will often go well beyond what infor-mants may talk about because much of their cultural knowledge is tacit. However, don't overlook the valuable insights and observations informants can give you.

CONTRAST QUESTIONS

As discussed in Step Four, the basic unit of all ethnographic inquiry is the *question-observation*. In order to make selective observations you will need to ask *contrast* questions, which are based on the differences that exist among the terms in each domain.

By now you have worked carefully with several cultural domains, each one a large category containing many smaller categories. You have identified cover terms and included terms, and you have looked for subsets among the included terms in your taxonomic analysis. All this search for the structure of cultural meaning has focused on the *similarities* among things. "What things are the same because they are all *kinds of witnesses*?" "What things are alike because they are all *stages in shopping*?" "What people are alike because they are all *kinds of customers*?"

However, the meaning of each cultural domain comes from the *differences* as well as the *similarities* among terms. Now we shift our attention to asking, "How are all these things different?" This approach is based on the principle of contrast, which states that cultural meaning is determined, in part, by how categories inside a domain contrast with one another. Any question that asks for differences is a contrast question. There are three types you can use in your research.

Dyadic Contrast Questions

A "dyad" refers to two items, a pair. A dyadic contrast question takes two members of a domain and asks, "In what ways are these two things different?"

Consider some examples. Earlier we identified several stages in shopping in a supermarket. A dyadic contrast question would ask: "What is the difference between *entering the store* and *checking out*?" The answer to this question can come from your own memory, from fieldnotes, or from making new *selected observations*. One difference immediately comes to mind: checking out always involves interaction between employee and customer, but entering the store almost never involves such interaction. You have identified a single difference between these two stages.

In his study of *Daytop Village*, Sugarman (1974) studied the roles people assumed during encounter groups. In studying this domain Sugarman developed nearly a dozen analytic categories, roles such as *identifier, preacher, reflector,* and *prosecutor*. This identification was based on recognition of the similarities among all these roles. In a search for differences it was necessary to ask numerous contrast questions: "What is the difference between identifier and preacher?" "What is the difference between identifier and reflector?" "What is the difference between preacher and prosecutor?" When you begin asking dyadic contrast questions you often discover there is much more information to collect in the field. Like all contrast questions, these always involve terms from the *same domain*. If you ask for differences among terms from different domains, the contrast is so large that it is seldom fruitful for ethnographic purposes.

Triadic Contrast Questions

This type of question uses three terms or categories at the same time. It takes the following form: "Which two are most alike in some way, but different from the third?" This kind of question involves looking for similarities and contrasts at the same time. It is especially useful for uncovering tacit contrasts that are easily overlooked.

Consider the following example. A colleague and I undertook a study of a restaurant that I shall call the Golden Nugget Night Club (Spradley and Schroedl 1972). We were interested in the interaction between employees and customers and the cultural rules for ordering food. In particular we wanted to know how people asked for different kinds of meat from the carver when they went through the food line. The carver's job was to slice pieces from a large round of roast beef. The amount of fat, the leanness of the slices, the number of slices, and their thickness were all determined by the carver in response to specific customer requests. During any evening of work the carver would engage in more than twenty-four distinct cultural activities such as *punching in, changing clothes, sharpening knives, setting up the line, trimming the round, serving the roast beef, taking a break,* and *watching the chips.* These were members of a domain, "kinds of activities of the carver." In our research we asked numerous contrast questions to discover the differences among all these activities. Here are two triadic contrast questions and some answers that will give you an idea of their nature.

1. Of these three, which two are most alike and which one is different: *sharpening knives, setting up the line, taking a break?*
   Answer: Setting up the line and taking a break are alike because most of the other employees do both of them also; sharpening knives is different because only the carver does that.
2. Of these three, which two are alike and which one is different: *sharpening knives, serving the roast beef, trimming the round?*
   Answer: Serving the roast beef and trimming the round are alike because they happen on the line; sharpening the knives happens in the kitchen.

Card-Sorting Contrast Questions

One of the easiest ways to get at the differences among the things in a cultural domain is to write them all on small cards and sort them into piles.

As you begin to go through the pile of cards, ask yourself: "Are there any differences among these things?" When you come to the first thing that appears different *for any reason at all,* place it in a new pile. Now you have two piles, and you can continue to sort the cards until you find one that doesn't fit either of the piles; then start a third, and so on. This technique for discovering contrasts works especially well when you have a large domain with many terms.

Consider the following domain. In my research with tramps I discovered they often slept outside, in old buildings and in dozens of other places. They referred to such places as "flops." Although most of my information on flops came from interviews with informants, I did some participant observation in places where I could observe tramps "making a flop." Before I finished examining the domain, "kinds of flops," I had discovered more than one hundred different types. Writing them on cards I could sort them into piles or ask an informant to assist me in sorting them. In either case, I began with a contrast question, "Is the next card different from the last one in some way?" Here are several piles that emerge from this type of procedure:

1. *Requires payment*
   flop house
   flea bag
   all-night theater
   hotel

2. *Doesn't require payment*
   graveyard
   sand house
   brick kiln
   weedpatch

3. *Other requirements besides money*
   mission flop
   the bucket

Card-sorting contrast questions enable you to deal with numerous terms at the same time. You find out similarities as well as differences.

Dimensions of Contrast

The differences you discover by asking contrast questions are called *dimensions of contrast.* In the last example, you saw three dimensions of contrast that can be rephrased as (1) requires money, (2) doesn't require money or anything else, (3) doesn't require money but does require something else. These dimensions of contrast are important facets of cultural meaning in the domain "kinds of flops."

In the contrast made earlier for "stages in shopping," one dimension of contrast that emerged was whether customers and employees interacted during a particular stage. The discovery of any dimension of contrast becomes the basis for making selective observations. For example, you could go back to the supermarket with a new question: "What kind of interaction occurs between customer and employee during each stage of shopping?'' As we turn to a discussion of selective observation, keep in mind that the question-observation unit, though made up of two distinct elements, must occur as a single, unitary process.

SELECTIVE OBSERVATIONS

It is useful to think of the three kinds of observation as a funnel. The broad rim of the funnel consists of *descriptive observations* in which you want to catch everything that goes on. These are the foundation of all ethnographic research and will continue throughout your entire project. Moving down from the mouth or rim, the funnel narrows sharply. *Focused observations* require that you narrow the scope of what you are looking for. But when you start this more focused type of investigation, you know what you are looking for—the categories that belong in a particular domain. You want to find all the "parts of a building" or "kinds of persons" or "stages in an activity." At the bottom of a funnel there is an extremely narrow, restricted opening. *Selective observations* represent the smallest focus through which you will make observations. They involve going to your social situation and *looking for differences among specific cultural categories*. There are at least three ways to look for these differences.

First, in those cases where you have not discovered any contrasts, you will want to look for any differences that exist. Let's say that you undertake a study of directory assistance operators by making numerous phone calls and asking for information. Soon it becomes apparent that there are several "kinds of operators." You identify the following types: *the impatient operator, the joker, the question asker, the novice,* and *the supervisor.* In addition to observations you ask your friends to relate the experiences they have had with different operators. Now you ask a contrast question of yourself: "What is the difference between a question asker and a novice?" You made these categories because you observed some difference, but now you cannot think of anything that contrasts them. Both ask questions, both work at about the same speed; you probably picked up some subtle difference that led you to using these categories. Now you must make focused observations or talk to informants some more *about this specific difference.*

Second, when you have discovered one or two differences, you may still need to discover more. Focused observations are used to extend your list of differences. We knew that the carver's activities at the Golden Nugget Night Club were different. Sharpening knives, for example, took place in the kitchen while trimming the round took place on the line. But what other differences exist between these two activities? With this contrast question in mind, focused observations led to at least the following: you could joke with other employees while sharpening knives, and it was also more fun.

Third, when you have discovered a dimension of contrast that applies to two or more terms in a domain, you may still need to find out if it applies to the other members of that domain. An important dimension of contrast for the domain "kinds of flops" had to do with whether the police would bother tramps or not. Once I discovered that some flops were defined by this fact and others were not, I needed to go through the entire list and find out whether this contrast applied or not.

Selective observations require careful planning. When you first go into the field to make observations you have only a few general questions. Now you will need to write out many specific contrast questions before you approach the social situation you are studying. It becomes increasingly necessary to make notes in the situation that answer each of your questions. And even with many specific questions in mind, you will want to make additional selective observations on the basis of a single, general inquiry: "What differences can I see for the members of this cultural domain?" Obviously it would be possible to continue searching for differences for a long time. For some domains you will want to be more exhaustive than others, but don't get trapped into the impossibility of finding out every possible difference or you will delay the completion of your project. As we turn to componential analysis in the next step we will discuss ways to organize the data collected from selective observations. In addition, this type of analysis will help you decide when you have collected enough specific information to move on to searching for themes and writing up your ethnography.

Tasks

8.1 Make a list of people with whom you might conduct informal or formal ethnographic interviews. Consider the value of supplementing your participant observation with ethnographic interviews.

8.2 Select one or more domains and ask yourself contrast questions to discover dimensions of contrast. Review your fieldnotes to answer these questions when needed.

8.3 Conduct a period of field investigation in which you add selective observations to the other two types used earlier.

OBJECTIVES
1. To understand the role of componential analysis in the study of cultural meaning systems.
2. To identify the steps in making a componential analysis.
3. To carry out a systematic componential analysis on one or more contrast sets.

Let's review briefly where the Developmental Research Sequence has brought us. First, our goal in ethnography is to discover the cultural patterns people are using to organize their behavior, to make and use objects, to arrange space, and to make sense out of their experience. You began by selecting a social situation and making undirected observations. Your first task was to collect samples of behavior, events, objects, and feelings. Your fieldnotes quickly grew in volume as a record of the "stream of human behavior" you observed.

But culture is a complex set of meaningful symbols that people have learned. This meaning system, whether tacit or explicit, is not immediately apprehended by the participant observer. And so you were introduced to a number of specific strategies for discovering the meaning in a cultural scene. First, you conducted a *domain analysis* and followed it up with *focused observations*. In doing this you took several important steps in discovering the *pattern,* the *organization* of cultural behavior, cultural artifacts, and cultural knowledge. Next, you undertook a *taxonomic analysis* and followed it up with more focused observations. Now you began to see the way several cultural domains were organized. Then we discussed the premise that cultural meaning comes not only from patterns based on similarity but also from patterns based on contrast. And so you narrowed your research focus even more and used *selective observations* to look for contrasts within several cultural domains.

At this point in the research there is a tendency to feel overwhelmed with the details of ethnographic fact. We saw how to organize and represent domains through taxonomic analysis, a process that helped simplify the data. Now we are ready to organize and represent all the contrasts you have discovered. This process, one you actually began in the last step, is called *componential analysis*.

COMPONENTIAL ANALYSIS

Componential analysis is the systematic search for the attributes (components of meaning) associated with cultural categories. Whenever an ethnographer discovers contrasts among the members of a domain, these contrasts are best thought of as attributes or components of meaning. A "component" is another term for "unit"; thus, componential analysis is looking for the units of meaning that people have assigned to their cultural categories.

Let's take a rather small domain, one I make use of every day. At the college where I teach I receive mail each day in a box with a combination lock on it. I visit my mailbox almost every day, open the lock, and remove a stack of paper envelopes and small packages. All the things put into that box are "mail." If someone from a culture without mail looked at the small pile of paper, he or she would have trouble seeing the differences that I see, for this pile is always made up of several different "kinds of mail." That cultural domain has at least the following smaller categories:

1. junk mail
   1.1. notices
   1.2. advertisements
   1.3. solicitations
2. bills
3. magazines
4. journals
5. books
6. newsletters
7. personal letters

These are all similar; they are kinds of mail. But they are also different. Each has a unique cluster of *attributes* that I have learned. The cultural meaning of each of these kinds of mail derives, in part, from these attributes. Two envelopes may appear identical on the outside, but I can scan the address, the return address, the stamp, and tell that one is probably a "bill" and the other a "personal letter." Once opened, I identify other attributes that clearly distinguishes one from the other.

An attribute is any element of information regularly associated with a cultural category. "Personal letters" have the attribute of "personal address," often using my first name. They also have the attribute of a signature from someone I recognize as an individual human being. "Bills," on the other hand, use neither personal address nor signature inside the envelopes. They are usually impersonal printed forms. In addition, they have the attribute of requesting payment for some kind of service or goods. The amount of payment is specified and the form is always money, not favors or food. All these different kinds of mail have many bits of cultural information attached to them that make them meaningful. It tells me to discard junk mail immediately but not personal letters or bills. It tells me how to feel and when

131

to act. When I open my mailbox each day I do not stop to think about this domain or the attributes of each kind of mail. I know them so well that I act on the tacit cultural meanings without thinking. Through participant observation in the mail room a competent ethnographer could discover this domain and the components of meaning (attributes) I associate with each small category of mail.

The attributes for all the cultural categories in a domain can be represented in a chart known as a *paradigm*. This simple device also will make the work of componential analysis easier and more systematic. Here is an example of a paradigm which uses three categories of mail.

DOMAIN	DIMENSIONS OF CONTRAST		
	Signed	*Action*	*Feeling*
junk mail	no	throw away	disgust
personal letters	yes	read and keep	delight
bills	no	read and pay	don't like

Through this paradigm I have shown some of the attributes for these three cultural categories: whether they are signed, the action I usually take after receiving each kind, and the feeling I have learned to associate with each kind of mail. This example paradigm doesn't exhaust the meaning; I present it only to show the nature of a paradigm. We can take out all this specific information and make clear the various features of a paradigm.

CULTURAL DOMAIN	DIMENSIONS OF CONTRAST		
	I	II	III
cultural category	$attribute_1$	$attribute_2$	$attribute_3$
cultural category	$attribute_1$	$attribute_2$	$attribute_3$
cultural category	$attribute_1$	$attribute_2$	$attribute_3$

The first column contains the members of a domain or some subset of a domain. If we take a single cultural category, the row of spaces opposite it contains the attributes associated with it. If we shift our attention from a single cultural category to all three (the entire column), each column of attributes becomes a dimension of contrast. This is any dimension of meaning on which some or all the cultural categories contrast. With this analytic tool you can make a componential analysis on any domain you have discovered in the cultural scene you are studying. Let's turn now to the specific steps you can go through to make a componential analysis.

STEPS IN MAKING A COMPONENTIAL ANALYSIS

A componential analysis includes the entire process of searching for contrasts, sorting them out, grouping some together as dimensions of contrast, and entering all this information onto a paradigm. It also includes verifying this information through participant observation or interviews. Although this may appear to be a complex process, you have already done much of the work involved.

In order to illustrate the specific steps necessary for making a componential analysis, I will draw on Starr's (1978) excellent study of ethnic groups in Lebanon. Lebanon is a country recently torn by strife among ethnic groups, groups not based on race or skin color but largely on religious affiliation. In many situations, such as purchasing a newspaper or selecting a taxi, the ethnic-group status of another person is not important. But in most of life's important events, ethnic-group membership is crucial. Starr wanted to know how people define the various ethnic groups and how people in everyday life were recognized as belonging to one or another group.

As we examine this study as an illustration of componential analysis we should not overlook another important characteristic. Up to now I have written about participant observation as if it were always conducted in a single social situation or a cluster of related social situations in an effort to simplify the research setting for the beginning ethnographer. By focusing on a single social situation and studying the cultural meanings in that situation you have been able to acquire numerous research skills. However, participant observation is a strategy that can be used in much larger settings. In his study Starr selected a particular problem and through participant observation studied the groups in an entire country. Of course, he did not participate and observe in all the activities that go on in Lebanon. Rather, he selected a sample of social situations that would yield information about the cues people use to recognize ethnic identity. He worked primarily in the capital city, Beirut, doing participant observation in such social situations as homes, cafés, public markets, shops, offices, pinball parlors, busses, and other public places. He interviewed informants, both informally and formally and asked a group of eighty-seven people to write essays on the topic of inferring the ethnic group of an unknown person. In all this research Starr focused almost exclusively on a single cultural domain: *kinds of ethnic groups*. In presenting the following steps, I do not mean to imply that he followed them in the precise sequence given below. All ethnography involves adapting strategies for use in particular situations. The following sequence will take any beginning ethnographer through componential analysis. Once understood, you may want to modify the procedures to fit your style of investigation.

Step One: Select a domain for analysis. For the first try at this kind of analysis you will find that a domain with less than ten included terms simplifies the task. However, select any domain for which you have collected contrasts. Here is a partial taxonomy of ethnic groups in Lebanon:

Ethnic Groups in Lebanon

1. Arabs
  1.1. Moslems
    1.11. Sunni
    1.12. Shi'ite
    1.13. Alawi
    1.14. Ismalili
  1.2. Druze
  1.3. Arab Christians
    1.31. Maronites
    1.32. Greek Orthodox
    1.33. Greek Catholics
    1.34. Protestants
    1.35. Latins
    1.36. Assyrians
    1.37. Chaldeans

2. Non-Arab Middle Easterners
  1.1. Armenians
    1.11. Armenian Apostolic
    1.12. Armenian Catholic
    1.13. Armenian Protestant
  1.2. Jews
  1.3. Kurds
  1.4. Gypsies

3. Foreigners
  1.1. Americans
  1.2. French
  1.3. Other Europeans
  1.4. Black Africans
  1.5. Japanese
  1.6. Indians/Pakistanis

Step Two: Inventory all contrasts previously discovered. You can begin with notes made from asking contrast questions and making selective observations. For example, Starr noted in observations that a Moslem male may have a religious tattoo that indicates the date of a pilgrimage to Mecca whereas a Christian male may have a cross inked on his skin. He also noted that Armenians and Kurds do not speak Arabic as their first language while most Moslems do. When these groups do speak Arabic, their accents will show marked differences.

Any statements about any cultural category in the domain you are analyzing can be used. Write down each contrast on a separate sheet of paper, thus compiling a list of contrasts. Here are some examples:

1. Kurds have first names that are Arab Islamic, Kurdish, or Nonspecific

Arab; Druze have first names that are Arab Islamic, Druze, or Nonspecific Arab.
2. Armenian Catholics speak Armenian as a first language; Shunni speak Arabic as a first language.
3. Greek Orthodox wear the Greek Cross as jewelry; Greek Catholics wear the Latin Cross and the St. Mary Medal.

Step Three: Prepare a paradigm worksheet. A paradigm worksheet consists of an empty paradigm in which you enter the cultural categories of the domain down the lefthand column. The worksheet should have attribute spaces large enough for you to write a number of words or short phrases. At the start of any componential analysis you will want to enter more information on the paradigm worksheet than will appear when it is completed. On a large worksheet you can make notes to yourself that show links between the paradigm and other domains. Figure 16 shows a paradigm worksheet on which some initial analysis has been done.

Step Four: Identify dimensions of contrast that have binary values. A dimension of contrast is an idea or concept that has at least two parts. For example, if you were analyzing the domain "kinds of trees," you would come up with one dimension of contrast that might be stated "characterized by the presence of leaves." This is a dimension of contrast related to trees and has two values or parts: (1) yes, a tree does have leaves; (2) no, a tree does not have leaves. This dimension of contrast has two (binary) values. You can often state this type of contrast dimension in the form of a question: "Does it have leaves?"

From the last example of contrasts, we can formulate a binary dimension of contrast: "Does member wear Greek Cross?" This dimension of contrast can now be entered at the top of one of the columns on the paradigm worksheet under DIMENSIONS OF CONTRAST. A second binary dimension might be "Speaks Armenian as first language." As you generate binary contrast dimensions, be sure to enter the values on your paradigm worksheet for the cultural categories you have data for. In most cases you can simply enter a "yes" or "no" or leave the space blank.

Step Five: Combine closely related dimensions of contrast into ones that have multiple values. The major reason for beginning with dimensions of contrast that have binary values (as in Figure 16) is their simplicity. However, almost always, two dimensions of contrast, each with binary values, will on closer inspection prove to be related. For example, in Figure 16 we have the following dimensions of contrast: (1) "Speaks Armenian as first language," (2) "Speaks Kurdish as first language," and (3) "Speaks Arabic as first language," and under each column I entered "yes" or "no" depending on applicability. Now we can combine these three columns into a *single*

135

FIGURE 16. Paradigm Worksheet: Partial Domain, "Kinds of Groups"

DOMAIN		Speaks Armenian as first language	Speaks Kurdish as first language	Speaks Arabic as first language	Does member wear Greek Cross?
Moslems	Shunni	no	no	yes	no
	Shi'ite	no	no	yes	no
Druze		no	no	yes	no
Arab Christians	Maronites	no	no	yes	no
	Greek Orthodox	no	no	yes	yes
	Greek Catholics	no	no	yes	no
	Assyrians	no	no	yes	yes
Armenians	Apostolics	yes	no	no	no
	Catholics	yes	no	no	no
Kurds		no	yes	no	no

DIMENSIONS OF CONTRAST

dimension of contrast which can be titled "First language." Now, rather than "yes" or "no," we can enter the first language of each group in the appropriate attribute space. Figure 17 is a second paradigm worksheet on which this type of combining has been done and on which several new dimensions of contrast have been added.

Sometimes the amount of information exceeds the space allowed on a paradigm worksheet. Also, on the final paradigm it may not be convenient to enter all the attributes possible because of space. One convention in such cases is to make use of numbers and list the attributes in a separate place. In Figure 17, one dimension of contrast is the source of a person's first name. There are numerous possibilities across ethnic groups and within each ethnic group. The numbered items in the attribute spaces of Figure 17 correspond to the following sources of first names:

1. Armenian
2. French
3. Anglo-Saxon
4. Maronite
5. Greek Orthodox
6. Arabic Christian
7. Arab Islamic
8. Druze
9. Shi'ite
10. Kurdish
11. Nonspecific Arab
12. Syriac- Aramaic

As you combine dimensions of contrast you may find it convenient to make use of this type of numbering system.

Step Six: Prepare contrast questions for missing attributes. One of the great values of a paradigm worksheet is that it will quickly reveal the kinds of information you need to collect. It offers a kind of check sheet that will guide you in preparing questions for future research. Every blank space or question mark can serve as a reminder that you need to search for missing attributes.

Step Seven: Conduct selective observations to discover missing information. In your search for additional ethnographic data, keep in mind that you may not find everything you want to know. There is nothing wrong with completing an ethnographic description that includes question marks or blank spaces in your paradigms. You will have to be the judge, in terms of the amount of time and interest, whether to pursue every contrast question until you have discovered an answer for all.

FIGURE 17. Paradigm Worksheet: Partial Domain, "Kinds of Groups"

DIMENSIONS OF CONTRAST

DOMAIN		First language	Men: tattoos or body scars	Women's dress	First name
Moslems	Shunni	Arabic	Islamic symbol	Western	7, 11
	Shi'ite	Arabic	Islamic symbol	Western	7, 9, 11
	Druze	Arabic	?	Western	7, 8, 11
Arab Christians	Maronites	Arabic	Cross, etc	Western	2, 3, 4, 6, 11
	Greek Orthodox	Arabic	Cross, etc	Western	3, 5, 6, 11
	Greek Catholic	Arabic	Cross, etc	Western	2, 3, 6, 11
	Assyrians	Arabic	Cross, etc	Western	6, 11, 12
Armenians	Apostolics	Armenian		Western	1, 2, 3
	Catholics	Armenian		Western	1, 2, 3
Kurds	Kurds	Kurdish	?	traditional	7, 10, 11

Step Eight: Prepare a completed paradigm. The final paradigm can be used as a chart in your ethnography. Although you will not be able to discuss every single attribute on the chart, you can discuss important ones and refer the reader to the chart. It allows you to present a large amount of information in a concise and orderly manner.

In this chapter I have presented the steps in making a componential analysis. In the study of any particular cultural scene you must decide which domains to examine in this kind of detail. Some ethnographers seek to make a componential analysis of as many domains as possible, while others limit this detailed investigation to one or more central domains, describing other aspects of a cultural scene in more general terms. I think it is advisable to examine at least two related domains in this intensive manner. We have now completed a discussion of in-depth ethnographic analysis. In the next step we will move back to the surface of a cultural domain to try and construct a more holistic view.

Tasks

9.1 Make a componential analysis of one or more domains, following the steps presented in this chapter.

9.2 Conduct a period of participant observation making use of all three types of observation: descriptive, focused, and selective.

DISCOVERING CULTURAL THEMES

OBJECTIVES
1. To understand the nature of cultural themes in doing ethnographic research.
2. To identify strategies for making a theme analysis.
3. To carry out a theme analysis on the cultural scene being studied.

The ethnographer must forever keep in mind that research proceeds on two levels at the same time. One examines small details of a culture and at the same time seeks to chart the broader features of the cultural landscape. An adequate cultural description will include an in-depth analysis of selected domains; it will also include an overview of the cultural scene and statements that convey a sense of the whole.

Some ethnographers convey a sense of the whole culture or cultural scene by what I call the *inventory approach*. They identify all the different domains in a culture, perhaps dividing them into categories like "kinship," "material culture," and "social relationships." Although a simple listing of all domains is a necessary part of ethnography, it is not sufficient. I believe it is important to go beyond such an inventory to discover the *cultural themes* that a society's members have learned and use to connect these domains. In this step we shall examine the nature of cultural themes and how they can be used to give us a holistic view of a culture or cultural scene.

CULTURAL THEMES

The concept of "cultural theme" was first introduced into social science by anthropologist Morris Opler, who used it to describe the general features of Apache culture. Opler proposed that we could better understand the general pattern of a culture by identifying recurrent themes. He defined a theme as "a postulate or position, declared or implied, and usually controlling behavior or stimulating activity, which is tacitly approved or openly promoted in a society" (1945:198). An example of a postulate he found expressed in many areas of Apache culture is the following: "Men are physically, mentally, and morally superior to women." Opler found this tacit premise expressed itself in the beliefs that women caused family fights, were more easily tempted sexually, and never assumed leadership roles in Apache society.

The concept of theme has its roots in the general idea that cultures are more than bits and pieces of custom. Rather, every culture is a complex pattern. In *Patterns of Culture* (1934), Benedict was the first to apply this idea to entire cultures. She examined the details of the Kwakiutl, Pueblo, and Dobuan cultures in search of general themes that organized these ways of life into dynamic wholes. For example, she saw the dominant pattern of Kwakiutl culture as one that emphasized the value of ecstasy, frenzy, and breaking the boundaries of ordinary existence. This theme, which Benedict called Dionysian, emerged again and again in dances, rituals, myths, and the routines of daily life. Although her analysis has been questioned, Benedict's important contribution was her insight into the nature of cultural patterning. Every culture, and every cultural scene, is more than a jumble of parts. It consists of a system of meaning that is integrated into some kind of larger pattern. Many other anthropologists have sought to capture this larger pattern with such concepts as values, value-orientations, core values, core symbols, premises, ethos, eidos, world view, and cognitive orientation.

For purposes of ethnographic research I will define a cultural theme as *any principle recurrent in a number of domains, tacit or explicit, and serving as a relationship among subsystems of cultural meaning.*

Cognitive Principle

Cultural themes are elements in the patterns that make up a culture. They will usually take the form of an assertion such as "men are superior to women," or "you can't beat a drunk charge." A cognitive principle is something that people believe and accept as true and valid; it is an assumption about the nature of their commonly held experience.

The assertions that comprise "what people know" differ in respect to their *generality*. One assertion common among the tramps I studied (Spradley 1970) was that "you can't trust a rubber tramp" (one who travels by car). This is a rather specific assertion, limited in its application to a single member (rubber tramps) of a single domain (kinds of tramps). Other assertions apply to a much larger realm of experience. For example, when a tramp says "You can't beat a drunk charge," he is making an assertion about a universal experience among tramps (getting arrested on a drunk charge), an assertion that would occur in many contexts (in and out of jail), and one that is related to many domains (ways to beat a drunk charge, kinds of time, stages in making the bucket, and the like).

Themes are assertions that have a high degree of generality. They apply to numerous situations and recur in two or more domains. One way themes can be detected is by examining the dimensions of contrast from several domains. Among tramps a recurring dimension of contrast had to do with the concept of *risk*. When contrasting all the different *kinds of flops*, tramps continually make reference to the risk of sleeping in one or another place. When a tramp says "Sleeping under a bridge is a good flop; *it's a call job*," he means the risk is low. Cops will probably not spot you there; someone must call them to tell them you are there. Again, in contrasting the different *ways to hustle* in jail, the amount of risk involved with each type emerged as a dimension of contrast. Likewise, in contrasting all the *ways to beat* a drunk charge, the degree of risk assigned to each one was an important dimension of contrast. When a single idea recurs in more than one domain such as this, it suggests the possibility of a cultural theme.

Let's take another example, this time from the culture of cocktail waitresses at Brady's Bar (Spradley and Mann 1975). Several domains were examined for contrasts, including *places in the bar, kinds of employees, kinds of drinks,* and *kinds of customers*. One dimension of contrast that emerged from making a componential analysis for each of these domains had to do with gender or sex. Waitresses distinguished the places in the bar in terms of male space and female space; they distinguished kinds of employees primarily by their gender; they distinguished drinks on the basis of male and female; customers also were divided up by male and female attributes. As we inspected these various domains, it became clear that an important aspect of cultural meaning was maleness and femaleness. A general principle or cultural theme emerged: *Life in this bar should clearly demarcate male and female realms*. Once we discovered this theme, we began looking for other specific instances of this general principle. It turned out that even very small domains like *ways to tip* and *ways to pay for drinks* clearly expressed the theme of gender.

It is important to recognize that cultural themes need not apply to *every* part of a culture. Some themes recur within a restricted context or only link two or three domains. Most ethnographers consider the search for a single, all-encompassing theme, as Benedict attempted to do, a futile one. It is more likely that a culture or a particular cultural scene will be integrated around a set of major themes and minor themes. In beginning to search for themes, the ethnographer must identify all that appear, no matter how broad their general application.

Tacit or Explicit

Cultural themes sometimes appear as folk sayings, mottoes, proverbs, or recurrent expressions. The Mae Enga, for example, who live in the highlands of New Guinea, recognize several themes related to pigs. Pigs are highly valued, symbolize status, are exchanged in important rituals, and frequently live in the houses with people. A common expression among the Mae Enga sums up this cultural theme: "Pigs are our hearts!" (Meggitt 1974). Tramps will readily state, "You can't beat a drunk charge." One ethnographer studied a Japanese bank whose official motto was "Harmony and Strength" (Rohlen 1974). This motto summed up a recurrent theme in the social structure and ritual activities of bank employees. Sometimes such explicit expressions of a theme do not contain the full principle; they do, however, provide clues that enable the ethnographer to formulate the cultural theme.

But most cultural themes remain at the *tacit* level of knowledge. People do not express them easily, even though they know the cultural principle and use it to organize their behavior and interpret experience. Themes come to be taken for granted, slipping into that area of knowledge where people are not quite aware or seldom find need to express what they know. This means that the ethnographer will have to make inferences about the principles that exist. Agar, in his study of heroin addicts, identified themes and also emphasized that they are frequently tacit. He analyzed numerous domains that involved events in the lives of heroin users.

Throughout the different events, then, there is a recurrent concern with "knowing the other." The principle involved might be characterized as: Assume that everyone is a potential danger unless you have strong evidence to the contrary. [This principle] was never articulated by any of the junkies who worked in the study, though it might have been by a reflective junkie philosopher talking about the life (1976:3-4).

In my own research with tramps many of the themes remained tacit, several of them emerging from the study of courtroom behavior and interviewing court officials. I was perplexed by the fact that the judges gave suspended sentences to those who had families, jobs, and other resources. Any man who had twenty dollars could bail out on a drunk charge and never appear in court at all. I talked to a judge about these practices at length, and he assured me that he released tramps with families, jobs, or other resources because he felt they had a better chance of stopping their drinking. Whatever the reasons, it became clear that some tacit themes ran through the sentencing practices in the court. I formulated these on the basis of many inferences from what the judge said, from observations in the court, and from interviews with tramps. I stated these tacit themes as rules to be followed when dealing with men charged with public drunkenness (Spradley 1971: 351-58):

RULE ONE: When guilty of public drunkenness, a man deserves greater punishment if he is poor.

RULE TWO: When guilty of public drunkenness, a man deserves greater punishment if he has a bad reputation.

RULE THREE: When guilty of public drunkenness, a man deserves greater punishment if he does not have a steady job.

These themes actually form part of the overlap in cultures between judges and tramps. In neither cultural scene are these themes entirely explicit;

143

indeed, among judges, they are often denied, but they still reflect the working tacit knowledge used to sentence public drunks.

Themes as Relationships

Themes not only recur again and again throughout different parts of a culture, but they also *connect* different subsystems of a culture. They serve as a general semantic relationship among domains. As we shall see when we discuss theme analysis, one way to discover domains is to look for the relationships among domains.

In studying Brady's Bar, several domains came to our attention early in the research: *ways to ask for a drink, hassles,* and *kinds of customers.* We discovered quite quickly that the female cocktail waitresses considered most of their hassles to come from female customers. Indeed, much to our surprise, we found that they dreaded waiting on female customers and constantly berated them when talking among themselves. After eliciting the terms in these domains and doing some intensive analysis, we began seeking relationships among the domains. A major theme emerged, one tacitly known to waitresses and customers but never expressed. This theme, related to the emphasis upon male and female differences in the bar, can be asserted as follows: *female customers consider the purchase of drinks an economic transaction, while male customers consider it an opportunity to assert their masculinity.* This theme began to link other domains together and made clear why waitresses often enjoyed the way males ordered drinks but not the way females did. When the men ordered they teased, complimented, and joked with the waitresses, calling attention to their own masculinity and to the intrinsic femininity of the waitresses. After such a transaction, the waitresses gained more than an order for drinks or a tip after serving; they received a kind of sexual affirmation, something that the simple economic exchange with female customers never offered.

In an earlier step I suggested that ethnographic analysis consisted of a search for (a) the parts of a culture, (b) the relationship among those parts, and (c) the relationship of the parts to the whole. In studying cultural domains and taxonomies, you have been searching for parts and their relationships. The search for themes involves identifying another part of every culture, those cognitive principles that appear again and again. But the search for themes is also a means for discovering the relationships among domains and the relationships of all the various parts to the whole cultural scene. In the remainder of this step I want to present a number of strategies for conducting a theme analysis.

STRATEGIES FOR MAKING A THEME ANALYSIS

The techniques for making a theme analysis are less well developed than those used in other types of analysis presented in this book. What follows is a listing of strategies I have gleaned from my own research, the work of other ethnographers, and suggestions from students. This area of cultural analysis invites the most experimentation on the part of the ethnographer.

Immersion

Immersion is the time-honored strategy used by most ethnographers. By cutting oneself off from other interests and concerns, by listening to informants hour on end, by participating in the cultural scene, and by allowing one's mental life to be taken over by the new culture, themes often emerge. Sometimes immersion broken up by brief periods of withdrawal generates insights into the themes of a culture. D'Andrade has called attention to this strategy as well as to the need for understanding how insights come to the ethnographer totally immersed in another society:

At present, the most frequently used (and perhaps most effective) technique for the study of cultural belief systems is for the individual ethnographer to immerse himself in the culture as deeply as possible and, by some series of private, unstated, and sometimes unconscious operations, to integrate large amounts of information into an organized and coherent set of propositions. To make these operations explicit, public, and replicable, or to develop a means of testing the accuracy of these operations, is likely to be a difficult and lengthy task. Nevertheless, it is a necessary task if the study of culture is to continue as a science (1976:179).

The ethnographer who has not gone to live in another society for a year or two can still make use of this strategy. For example, if you have been conducting participant observation for several hours each week over a period of several months, see if you can't immerse yourself for several days. Find a block of time and spend entire days and evenings in the social situation looking for cultural themes. After that, set aside a day or two to review your fieldnotes in an intensive manner. This type of immersion will often reveal new relationships among domains and bring to light cultural themes you cannot discover any other way.

Make a Componential Analysis of Cover Terms for Domains

From your investigation thus far you have developed a list of cultural domains. They actually form a large domain which you can tentatively call "domains in the cultural scene." Once you have shifted your attention to this larger set of cultural categories, you can use the same tools of analysis. Examine all the domains to see if they might fit into a taxonomy, thus grouping some together as subsets. Then, asking contrast questions, you can search for major differences among these domains. For example, in my own research on a small factory which makes tannery equipment, I reviewed many pages of fieldnotes and came up with the following list of domains:

1. Kinds of people	22. Parts of the valley
2. Kinds of jobs	23. Parts of the day
3. Kinds of machines	24. Times of the day
4. Kinds of hardware	25. Times of the week
5. Kinds of tools	26. Times of the year
6. Kinds of wood	27. Ways to talk
7. Kinds of tanneries	28. Ways to fuck off
8. Kinds of drums	29. Ways to prevent accidents
9. Kinds of jobs	30. Ways to get fired
10. Kinds of accidents	31. Ways to work
11. Steps in making a lunch run	32. Ways the boss gets down on you
12. Steps in making a drum	33. Places to deliver
13. Steps in making a vat	34. Places to pick up
14. Steps in making a paddlewheel	35. Places to go after work
15. Steps in getting hired	36. Things to talk about
16. Steps in getting fired	37. Things you eat
17. Reasons for taking time off	38. Things you do after work
18. Reasons for working at the valley	39. Things you can't do at work
19. Reasons for quitting	40. Things people do
20. Reasons for assigning jobs	41. Things people make
21. Reasons for fucking off	

This list of domains represents hundreds of included terms, some of which I had identified; others were still undiscovered at the time I made this list. A large paradigm worksheet would list all these domains down the lefthand column and a search for contrasts would begin.

Cultural themes function as general relationships among cultural domains. One way to search for themes, then, is to look for similarities and contrasts among domains such as this. Here is one contrast:

1. kinds of people
2. steps in making a lunch run
3. steps in making a drum

The first two domains are quite distinct from the third in that they are learned *informally*. Steps in making a drum is a complex routine that someone has to teach the beginning employee at this factory. Now I can examine all the other domains with this dimension of contrast in mind—how one learns the domain. This in turn suggests that there may be conflicts between activities learned informally and those learned formally.

A componential analysis of all known domains within a cultural scene focuses your attention on the scene *as a whole*. Another way to accomplish this broad perspective is to compare cultural scenes. This is another strategy for discovering cultural themes.

Search for a Larger Domain That Includes the Cultural Scene

In a complex society any particular cultural scene may belong to a class of cultural categories that are similar. For example, if you studied the cultural scene of a supermarket, you would know that it belonged to a much larger domain: kinds of stores. Without much additional research you might be able to identify the following members of this domain: *department stores, super-markets, discount houses, ma-and-pa groceries, clothing stores, co-ops,* and *hardware stores.* Once having created this larger domain, you could proceed with a componential analysis. The ways in which a supermarket contrasts with these other kinds of stores would tell you some very general things about supermarkets.

In the study mentioned earlier about the role of the carver at the Golden Nugget Night Club (Spradley and Schroedl 1972), we wanted to gain this overall perspective. In talking to restaurant people with long experience and drawing on our own observations, we identified the domain "kinds of res-taurants" and more than a dozen subcategories. One large part of the domain was called "fancy restaurants" and included the Golden Nugget Night Club. We then did a componential analysis on the six kinds of fancy restaurants which revealed important information about the scene we were studying. Figure 18 shows that analysis. We could quickly see that the menu was general rather than specialized; the Golden Nugget offered many salads and several different meats and vegetables, but steak or Chinese food could not be gotten. This fact helped us see the role of the carver in the context of the Golden Nugget as it contrasted with other types of restau-rants.

One can go further and compare a single domain within one cultural scene with similar ones in other cultures. This often suggests themes. For exam-ple, in studying cocktail waitresses, we observed that a pattern of joking occurred between waitresses and bartenders. It had so many similarities with the widespread "joking relationship" in non-Western societies that we examined the ethnographic literature and discovered themes that were ap-plicable to Brady's Bar (Spradley and Mann 1975:87-100).

Search for Similarities among Dimensions of Contrast

Another strategy for discovering cultural themes is the examination of the dimensions of contrast for all the domains that have been analyzed in detail. The dimensions of contrast represent a somewhat more general concept than the individual attributes associated with a term. Themes are more general

FANCY RESTAURANTS	DIMENSIONS OF CONTRAST			
	Type of menu	Private membership	Type of entertainment	Liquor served
Night club (Golden Nugget)	general	yes	"name"	yes
Specialty food restaurant	specialized	no	music	yes
Supper club	general	no	music	yes
Dinner theater	general	no	live play	yes
Steak house	specialized	no	music/none	varies
Family restaurant	general	no	none	no

FIGURE 18. Kinds of Fancy Restaurants

still, but dimensions of contrast can sometimes serve as a bridge between the most specific terms and their attributes and the themes that relate subsystems of cultural meaning.

I mentioned earlier how the dimensions of contrast that had to do with "risks" in the culture of tramps suggested possible themes about the insecurity of their daily lives. Let me give another example of dimensions of contrast. As I began to make a componential analysis of the different folk terms included in *tramp,* I thought contrasts like the amount of drinking or age might be important. Instead, almost all the dimensions of contrast were associated with mobility. My informants distinguished among all the different kinds of tramps in terms of (1) their degree of mobility, (2) their mode of travel, (3) the type of home base they had when traveling, and (4) the survival strategies employed when on the road. (See Spradley 1970:65-96 for an extended discussion of this domain.) When I examined the dimensions of contrast that tramps used to distinguish kinds of trusties (inmates) a similarity appeared. The different kinds of trusties were contrasted in terms of their mobility in and out of jail, down to very small degrees. Outside trusties had the most mobility, but even here some had less and were required to return to the jail each night or at noon and again at night. Those trusties who worked inside the jail were distinguished in terms of the degree of freedom they had to move around inside the jail. I concluded that something I called "mobility" was very much a part of the identities of my informants, both as tramps and as inmates in the jail. I then began to look for other evidence of mobility and how it might be important in the lives of tramps. It turned out that mobility was directly related to drinking behavior. When a tramp travels he leads a somewhat isolated life. Arriving in a new town and in need of human companionship, a spot job, or other resources, he heads for skid row and the bars. Bars are classified into more than a dozen different kinds in terms of the resources they provide. To a tramp, they are like churches, social clubs, employment agencies, and the welfare office, all rolled into one. But they are also places for drinking and as such reinforce the symbolic value of drinking to tramps. Without going into more detail, I soon discovered that the courts, missions, and even the alcoholism treatment center reinforced the tramps' desire to travel. The theme of mobility emerged as one of the most important in the entire culture of what I came to call "urban nomads." I originally discovered this theme by comparing the dimensions of contrast between two domains.

Identify Organizing Domains

Some domains in a cultural scene appear to organize a great deal of information in a dynamic fashion. This is particularly true of those based on the semantic relationship "X is a stage of Y." One of the most useful strategies for discovering cultural themes is to select an organizing domain for intensive analysis. In her study of directory assistance operators Ehrman (1977) selected two domains to organize most of the data collected. One was "stages in a typical day," the other "stages in a directory assistance call." Although a typical call lasted only a few seconds, it could be broken down into thirteen basic stages repeated over and over throughout the day.

One of the best kind of organizing domains are events, or a series of related events. Agar (1973), in his ethnography of heroin users, has shown the power of analyzing events and their interrelationships. In studying the culture of the Seattle City Jail from the perspective of inmates, I selected the domain "stages in making the bucket" as the major organizing domain. I was able to place this domain as a central focus of the ethnography. Then, as I described each stage in detail, I easily connected other domains to this one. For example, at each stage in the process, informants talked about smaller events encoded by verbs for action or activities. Organizing domains were discussed in Step Six, and at that point you may have selected one for investigation. If so, you can now examine it in relation to others to discover cultural themes.

Make a Schematic Diagram of the Cultural Scene

Another strategy for discovering cultural themes is to try and visualize relationships among domains. Figure 19 is a schematic diagram of the

FIGURE 19. Stages in Making the Bucket

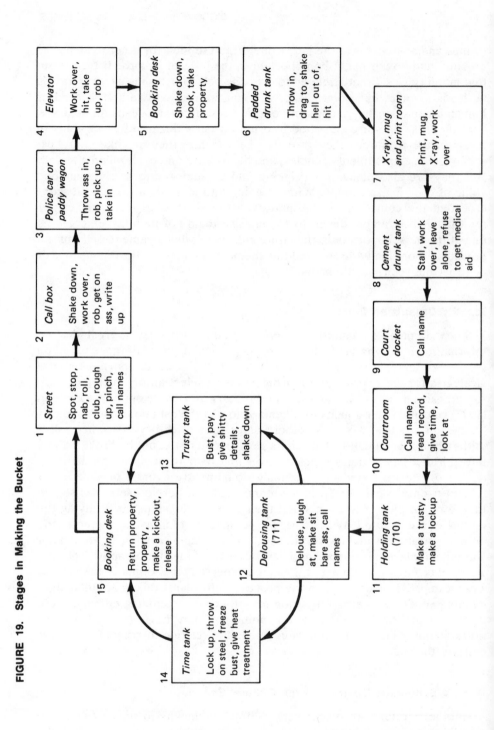

places tramps find themselves as they go through the "stages in making the bucket." It also includes information about the events that occur during this process. Although it doesn't begin to represent the entire cultural scene, even this partial diagram suggested many relationships and themes in this culture.

One can begin making schematic diagrams by selecting a limited number of domains and themes. For example, in Figure 20 I have shown some of the relationships that occur between the theme of mobility in tramp culture and various aspects of their lives. The final diagram you create is not nearly as important as the process of visualizing the parts of a cultural scene and their relationships. This thinking process is one of the best strategies for discovering cultural themes. Some of the diagrams you create may find their way into your final ethnographic description, helping to make clear the relationships to those who read the report.

In addition to making diagrams of limited aspects of the cultural scene and larger ones that attempt to encompass the entire scene, it is useful to go beyond the scene you are studying. A simple square or circle in the center of a sheet of paper can represent the entire cultural scene you have been studying. Then, with various sorts of lines to show the relationships, additional symbols can be used to represent other scenes within the wider culture or even other cultures. For example, the culture of tramps is connected to at least the following: their families, judges, the police department, the welfare office, the liquor stores, the religious missions, the junkyard dealers, the railroads and their employees, farmers, social scientists, and many more. By creating a diagram of all these possible other scenes that connect to the

FIGURE 20. Mobility and Drinking

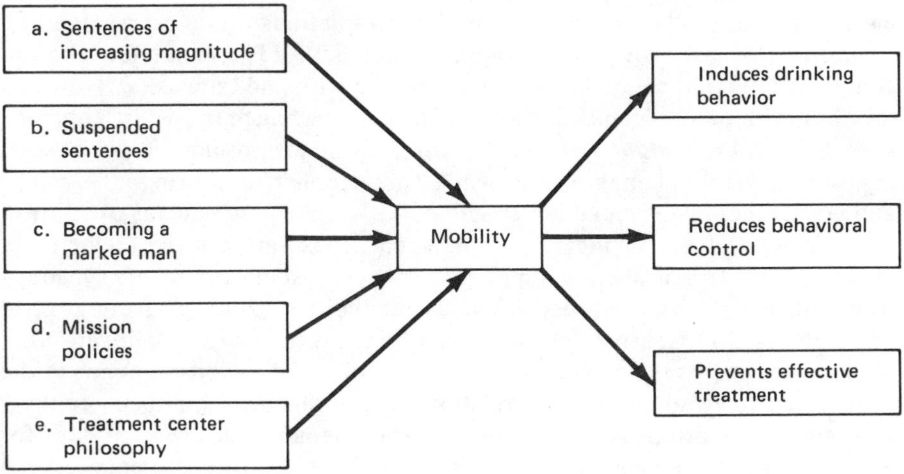

From Spradley 1973:29

world of tramps, I could see areas for future research and gain insights into the culture of tramps itself.

Search for Universal Themes

In the same way that there appear to be universal semantic relationships, there appear to be some universal cultural themes, the larger relationships among domains. The ethnographer who has a familiarity with universal themes may use them as a basis for scrutinizing the data at hand. The following list is a tentative, partial inventory of some universal or nearly universal themes that ethnographers have identified. Many more could be discovered by going through ethnographic studies and the literature of the social sciences. This list is merely intended to be suggestive of possible themes that might be found in the scene you are studying.

1. *Social conflict*. In every social situation conflicts arise among people, and these conflicts often become worked into cultural themes in ways that organize cultural meaning systems. Looking for conflicts among people is a useful strategy in studying any society. Tramps are in conflict with the police and this condition shows up in most of the domains in the culture. It is clearly related to the *risks* they take in the course of daily life.

2. *Cultural contradictions*. Cultural knowledge is never entirely consistent in every detail. Most cultures contain contradictory assertions, beliefs, and ideas. Lynd, in his classic analysis of American culture (1939), proposed twenty fundamental values or themes, most of which stood in opposition to others. For example, one stated, "Honesty is the best policy, but business is business and a businessman would be a fool if he did not cover his hand." One cultural contradiction that occurs in many cultural scenes has to do with the official "image" people seek to project of themselves, and the "insiders view" of what really goes on. Cultural contradictions often are resolved by *mediating themes*. Every ethnographer is well advised to search for inherent contradictions that people have learned to live with and then ask, "How can they live with them?" This may lead to the discovering of important themes.

3. *Informal techniques of social control*. A major problem in every society is the control of behavior, the need to get people to conform to the values and norms that make social life possible. Although formal means of control, such as police force or incarceration, occur, these are not the major techniques of control a society employs. In every society and every social situation, people have learned informal techniques that effectively control what others do. Gossip and informal social rewards are two means that function as mechanisms of control. By examining the various domains in the culture you have studied to find relationships to this need for social control, you may well discover important cultural themes. In Brady's Bar, for example, waitresses will seek to control the behavior of customers. Some-

times, when pinched or embraced, a waitress will go so far as to kick or verbally abuse a male customer, but most of the time more subtle, informal strategies are used. In an excellent study of tipping in another bar, Carlson (1977) has shown how waitresses control the tipping behavior of customers with subtle reminders such as leaving the change on the tray and then holding the tray at eye level. If the customer reaches for it, he will appear awkward and the waitress can quickly lower the tray and say, "Oh, I thought that was a tip."

4. *Managing impersonal social relationships.* In many urban settings, impersonal social relationships make up a major part of all human contact. In almost any urban cultural scene people have developed strategies for dealing with people they do not know. This theme may recur in various domains of the cultural scenes. In an excellent discussion of this nearly universal theme, Lofland (1973) has shown how it operates in many urban scenes.

5. *Acquiring and maintaining status.* Every society has a variety of status and prestige symbols, which people often strive to achieve and to maintain once they are achieved. We quickly think of money or athletic skill, but in every cultural scene there are status symbols, many of which are more subtle. Appearing "cool" under pressure may give one status; expressing a high degree of religious devotion confers status in some scenes. Cultural domains often reflect the status system of a culture and can become the basis for one or more major cultural themes.

6. *Solving problems.* Culture is a tool for solving problems. Ethnographers usually seek to discover what problems a person's cultural knowledge is designed to solve. For example, much of what tramps know appears to be aimed at solving a limited set of problems: making a flop, acquiring clothes, getting enough to eat, beating a drunk charge, escaping loneliness, finding excitement, and "making it" (acquiring resources such as money or alcoholic beverages). One can relate many of the domains in the culture of tramps by showing how each is related to the problems tramps are trying to solve. This same approach can be used in the study of almost any cultural scene.

In looking for universal cultural themes, a rich source lies in fiction. The themes in a novel often reflect universal cultural themes and by examining them carefully one can find clues to themes in the cultural scene being studied. For example, Joanne Greenberg has written an excellent novel about deaf people in the United States called *In This Sign*. A number of themes run through this novel, such as "sign language is a symbol of membership in the deaf community," and "sign language is a stigma among hearing people." Anyone doing ethnographic research among the deaf would find this novel a rich source of possible cultural themes that relate many domains.

153

Write a Summary Overview of the Cultural Scene

This strategy for discovering cultural themes will help to pull together the major outlines of the scene you are studying. In several brief pages, write an overview of the cultural scene for someone who has never heard about what you are studying. Include as many of the major domains as you can as well as any cultural themes you have identified. The goal of this overview is to condense everything you know down to the bare essentials. In the process of writing this kind of summary, you will be forced to turn from the hundreds of specific details and deal primarily with the larger parts of the culture; this, in turn, will focus your attention on the relationships among the parts of the culture and lead to discovering cultural themes.

In this chapter we have examined the concept of cultural theme and presented some strategies for discovering cultural themes. Every ethnographer will be able to develop additional ways to gain insights into the cultural themes that make up part of the tacit knowledge informants have learned. Each of the strategies discussed here will best be viewed as tentative guides to discovering cultural themes, not as a series of steps that inevitably lead to themes. Immersion in a particular culture still remains one of the most proven methods of finding themes. One way to gain a greater immersion into the ideas and meanings of a culture is to begin writing a description of that culture. Many ethnographers delay writing in the hope that they will discover new themes or complete their analysis in a more detailed manner. But writing the ethnographic description is best seen as part of the process of ethnographic discovery. As you write, new insights and ideas for research will occur. Indeed, you may find that writing will send you back for more ethnographic research to fill gaps in the data and test new hypotheses about cultural themes.

Tasks

1. **Identify as many cultural themes as you can by means of the strategies presented in this chapter and any others you find useful.**
2. **State all the cultural themes as brief assertions.**

OBJECTIVES
1. To identify the types of information you have collected.
2. To identify gaps in the information you have collected.
3. To begin to organize your data for writing the ethnography.

The fieldnotes created by an ethnographer as a record of research grow with amazing rapidity. After eight or ten sessions of making observations, then expanding on the notes taken in the field, beginning ethnographers sometimes have between seventy-five and a hundred pages of notes. Those who spend more hours in the field or supplement observations with interviews will have even more. In addition, you have created many pages of analysis—lists of ethnographic questions, lists of domains, individual domains with included terms, taxonomies, paradigm worksheets, and notes made while searching for themes. Even though you created all this material, the weeks have flown by since your first decision to study a particular social situation, and much has been forgotten.

But now it is time to begin organizing your material in preparation for writing the ethnography. You cannot memorize everything recorded in your field notebook, but you do need to have access to everything in order to make selections to be included in the final report. Some beginning ethnographers begin writing and use a retrieval method we can call "thumb through your fieldnotes." They begin by drawing on memory; then they "thumb through" page after page in search of an example, a theme, a map, or a domain. Sometimes they will recall an incident that occurred during their third week of research and quickly find it. At other times they will search through every page without success.

Before you begin the serious business of writing the ethnography, consider the value of taking a *cultural inventory*. By taking several hours to review all your notes— condensed accounts, expanded accounts, journal, analysis and interpretation—and recording what you have collected, you will actually save time. It will help you see the cultural scene as a whole. It will identify gaps in your research that can be easily filled. And most of all, by taking a systematic inventory you will discover ways to organize your final paper. In fact, although the next step deals with ethnographic writing, taking a cultural inventory can be considered part of it. In this step I want to suggest some strategies for making such an inventory.

Begin by selecting some place to record everything you have collected. You might want to use several pages at the front of your field notebook, or you might find that 4 × 6 cards will be the most convenient. One of the most effective ways to record an inventory involves using a large sheet of paper or even cardboard. When you record everything on a single large sheet, you can quickly scan that sheet as you write, keeping all the different kinds of ethnographic data in front of you. I know a student who used a large sheet of cardboard. After identifying the various kinds of data through a cultural inventory, she then placed it over her desk as she began writing. When she made note cards about examples or points to include in the report, she taped or pinned them to the cardboard, thus having ready access to them as the need arose. Select a system that is workable and will keep you from getting lost in your own data.

MAKE A LIST OF CULTURAL DOMAINS

In Step Five you made a list of as many cultural domains as you could from your fieldnotes. You have probably gone over your notes on more than one occasion since then to add to the list. Now you need to repeat this task. Begin by compiling a single list of all the domains you have located thus far, writing only the cover terms on your inventory page. Then go back to the first page of your expanded fieldnotes and skim through each page quickly, looking for domains you overlooked earlier. Look over the list of "general cultural domains" presented in Step Six to see if they might sensitize you to any additional possibilities. Leave room to add to this list since taking the rest of your cultural inventory will likely turn up a few.

MAKE A LIST OF ANALYZED DOMAINS

Look through the *analysis and interpretation* sections of your field notebook to find which domains you have analyzed. It helps to list analyzed domains in several different categories:

1. *Complete*: those domains for which you have worked out a taxonomy and a paradigm.
2. *Partial*: those domains for which you have done a partial taxonomic and componential analysis.
3. *Incomplete*: those domains for which you have cover term and some included terms, but which lack any systematic analysis.

In all probability the first and second categories of analyzed domains represent your ethnographic focus. If not, you might want to identify that focus in a separate place in your inventory.

COLLECT SKETCH MAPS

Every social situation holds many possibilities for sketch maps. In a study of a supermarket, for example, it would be possible to draw a detailed sketch map of the entire store. Then, even more detailed maps could be drawn of the check-out counter and other strategic areas. You may have drawn a map that shows the physical features and the routes people travel most frequently. Another map might show the same physical features but this time locate the most common activities and where they occur.

Sketch maps can include more than physical space. For example, you might sketch sequences of ritual activity or complex machinery that people work with. A network of friends or other relationships can be sketched or charted. Go through your fieldnotes and identify all the sketch maps you have already drawn. Then make a list of all the maps *you could possibly draw*. Your inventory should include both what you have and possibilities that might be worth including.

MAKE A LIST OF THEMES

List all the major and minor themes you have discovered. Those which are tentative can be listed but mark them as ones needing more investigation. Place all the themes together on a single page or at one place on a large inventory sheet.

INVENTORY EXAMPLES

An example is a description of some concrete event or experience. Examples begin with phrases like, "This morning I saw two men start to argue and . . . ." or "The following incident happened about 11:30 . . . ." An example always gives details, specifics about something that happened. Your final written ethnography will contain many examples, for they will bring your analysis to life and make it meaningful to the reader. All the domains and categories you have analyzed represent the skeleton of a cultural scene; examples put flesh on that skeleton.

Go back to the first page of your fieldnotes and skim through looking for examples. Some may only be a few lines long, others may run on for several pages. Try to give them a name or short descriptive phrase so you can make a list for your inventory. You will want to look especially for examples that are related to those domains you plan to write about in your final paper.

Some ethnographers get to this point in their inventory and discover that their fieldnotes have almost no examples. Instead of describing events in detail, they wrote things down in an abstract fashion. If you find yourself short on examples, take some time to make a list of ones you remember well enough to describe. Then, make another list of the kinds of examples you think you might need and could get by going back for more research.

Examples often look like stories. A good set of fieldnotes includes dozens of anecdotes, stories, incidents, and happenings. They are the kind of things ethnographers tell their friends after a period of fieldwork. "You know, a funny thing happened today . . . ."

IDENTIFY ORGANIZING DOMAINS

Look over your list of domains and see if any of them can serve as organizing domains. Such a domain will tie together many facets of a cultural scene. You will recall that earlier I suggested the domain "stages in shopping" was an organizing domain as well as "stages in making the bucket." Each one provides a lot of hooks on which to hang the rest of the cultural scene. If you have one or more organizing domains, write out the cover term and the major included terms so you can see the main structure. Such domains often become the backbone of an ethnography, and as you look over your inventory with an eye to outlining your paper, the organizing domains will be of great help.

MAKE AN INDEX OR TABLE OF CONTENTS

This can be as simple or elaborate as you think will be useful. Go through your fieldnotes and identify first the main categories, then look through each one and mark down the page numbers of the contents. Your expanded notes are arranged chronologically and you can probably identify the major topics on a page or every few pages. Sometimes it is worth the time to put the page numbers by each domain and each example you have found. Then later, when you need to draw on these for writing purposes, you won't have to search through every page.

INVENTORY MISCELLANEOUS DATA

In addition to fieldnotes from your observations, you may have additional information. In studying a first-grade classroom, you may have picked up lesson plans, student worksheets, and memos being sent home with students. During a study of air traffic controllers you might have come across an article in the newspaper about local conflicts between the union and airline companies. You may have taken photographs, discovered magazine articles, and even found artifacts related to the cultural scene. All these things can help in drafting your final paper. Identify them simply as "miscellaneous data" and place the list along with the rest of your inventory.

ADDITIONAL RESEARCH POSSIBILITIES

A final part of your inventory is to list future research possibilities in the cultural scene or outside of it which appear related to the research you have completed. A simple listing of topics can help to clarify the boundaries of the work you have done and make you aware of the limitations of your own work. Every ethnography is a partial ethnography, but in the course of immersion in the details of ethnographic data it is easy to lose sight of the edges of your work. If you plan to continue ethnographic research after writing up a first report, this list can become a valuable source for future decisions about what to study.

Taking a cultural inventory not only gives you an overall record of data collected, it also influences your thinking about the cultural scene. It is an effective way to review the work you have done and prepare to write it up.

Tasks

11.1 Review your fieldnotes and take a cultural inventory using the suggestions given in this step.

11.2 List the specific things you still want to find out from additional participant observation.

11.3 Conduct a period of field observation to fill any gaps in your data.

Step Twelve

WRITING AN ETHNOGRAPHY

OBJECTIVES
1. To understand the nature of ethnographic writing as part of the translation process.
2. To identify different levels of ethnographic writing.
3. To identify the steps in writing an ethnography.
4. To write an ethnography.

Every ethnographer probably begins the task of writing a cultural description with the feeling it is too early to start. Doing ethnography always leads to a profound awareness that a particular cultural meaning system is almost inexhaustibly rich. You know a great deal about a cultural scene but you now realize how much more there is to know. It is well to recognize that what you write is true of every ethnographic description: it is partial, incomplete, and will always stand in need of revision. Most ethnographers would do well to set aside the feelings that writing is premature and begin the task sooner rather than later. In the process of writing one discovers a hidden store of knowledge gained during the research process.

As most professional writers will affirm, the only way to learn to write is *to write*. In the same way that learning to swim cannot occur during classroom lectures on swimming, discussion of principles and strategies to follow in writing do not take one very far in learning to write. It is best to observe other swimmers, get in the water yourself and paddle around, and then have an experienced swimmer point out ways to improve your breathing and stroke.

One of the best ways to learn to write an ethnography is to read other ethnographies. Select those that communicate to you the meaning of another culture. Those written in a way that brings that culture to life, making you feel you understand the people and their way of life. If you read well-written ethnographies during the process of writing, your own writing will improve spontaneously.

Every ethnographer can identify books and articles that are well-written cultural descriptions. In the past eight years, my colleague David McCurdy and I have scoured the professional literature in search of brief examples of ethnographic writing of the highest caliber. Our standard has been to identify writing that translates the meanings of an alien culture so well that someone unfamiliar with ethnography grasps those meanings. These selections of ethnographic writing have been collected in three successive editions of *Conformity and Conflict: Readings in Cultural Anthropology* (1971, 1974, 1977). For sheer readability, two of the best longer ethnographies are Elliot Liebow's urban ethnography, *Tally's Corner* (1967), and Colin Turnbull's study of the Pygmies, *The Forest People* (1962).

In this step I want to examine briefly the nature of ethnographic writing as part of the translation process. Then I want to discuss the principles of the D.R.S. Method as applied to writing an ethnography. In the process I will give some specific suggestions on writing, but always keep in mind that the way to learn to write an ethnography is to write an ethnography.

THE TRANSLATION PROCESS

A translation discovers the meanings in one culture and communicates them in such a way that people with another cultural tradition can understand them. The ethnographer as translator has a dual task. For one, you must make sense out of the cultural patterns you observe, decoding the messages in cultural behavior, artifacts, and knowledge. The more fully you apprehend and digest the cultural meaning system operating in the social situation you study, the more effective your final translation.

Your second task is to *communicate* the cultural meanings you have discovered to readers who are unfamiliar with that culture or cultural scene. This means that every ethnographer must develop the skills of communicating in written form. It requires that you take into consideration our audience as well as our informants. In a real sense, a truly effective translation requires an intimate knowledge of two cultures: the one described and the one tacitly held by the audience who will read the description.

Many highly skilled ethnographers fail to finish the work of ethnographic translation. They give months of time to the intensive study of another culture, analyzing in great detail the meanings encoded in that culture. Then, without taking time to learn the skills of written communication, without understanding their audience, without even feeling the importance of communicating in a way that brings the culture to life, they write an ethnography. Their audience becomes a very small group of other ethnographers, who, by virtue of their interest in the culture, are willing to wade through the vague and general discussions, examine the taxonomies, paradigms, and other tables or charts, and glean an understanding of the people and their way of life. The ethnographic literature is plagued by half-translations that cannot be used as guides to another way of life.

In discussing the steps in writing an ethnographic description I will make numerous suggestions for creating a full translation, one that communicates the cultural meanings you have discovered. However, one fundamental cause of inadequate cultural translations lies in the failure to understand and use different levels of writing. During the writing of any ethnographic description, the ethnographer must keep these various levels in mind and consciously use them to increase the communicative power of the translation.

Levels of Ethnographic Writing

Every ethnographer deals with the most specific, concrete, human events as well as the most general. In our fieldnotes we identify an infant with a specific name, held by a specific mother, nursing at that mother's breast, at a specific time and in a specific place. In those same fieldnotes we will make observations about human love, nurturance, and the universal relationship of mothers and children. In the final written ethnography, the range of levels is enormous. More than anything else, the way these levels are used will determine the communicative value of an ethnographic translation.

Kenneth Read, in his beautifully written ethnography of the Gahuku peoples of Highland New Guinea, *The High Valley* (1965), suggests the underlying cause of partial translations in ethnography:

Why, then, is so much anthropological writing so antiseptic, so devoid of anything that brings a people to life? There they are, pinned like butterflies in a glass case, with the difference, however, that we often cannot tell what color these specimens are, and we are never shown them in flight, never see them soar or die except in generalities. The reason for this lies in the aims of anthropology, whose concern with the particular is incidental to an understanding of the general (1965:ix).

In anthropology, as in all social sciences, *the concern with the particular is incidental to an understanding of the general*. But when this principle is transported wholesale into doing ethnography, it creates a travesty of the translation process. When an ethnographer studies another culture, the only place to begin is with the particular, the concrete, specific events of everyday life. Then, through the research process described in this book, the ethnographer moves to more and more general statements about the culture. With the discovery of more general categories and cultural themes, the ethnographer begins to make comparisons with other cultures and make even more general statements about the culture studied. And all too frequently, it is primarily this kind of analysis and understanding that finds its way into the ethnographic description.

In writing an ethnography, as a translation in the full sense, *the concern with the general is incidental to an understanding of the particular*. In order for a reader to see the lives of the people we study, we must *show them through particulars*, not merely talk about them in generalities.

There are at least six different levels that can be identified in ethnographic writing as we move from the general to the particular. Let's examine each of these different kinds of translation statements.

162

Level One: Universal Statements

These include all statements about human beings, their behavior, culture, or environmental situation. They are all-encompassing statements. Although the beginning ethnographer may often feel incompetent to make any universal statements, all of us know things that occur universally and can include them in our ethnographies. Most cultural descriptions include universal statements. A study of air traffic controllers, for example, might assert, "In all societies, people manage the movement of their bodies through space in such a way that they do not constantly collide with other human beings." Such a statement is relevant to controlling the movement of vehicles in which humans move about as well. A study of clerks who record burglaries in the police department might assert the following universal statement: "In all human societies, some people keep records of one sort or another about their affairs."

For each of the six levels of abstraction that appear in ethnographic writing, I want to give an example from *The Cocktail Waitress: Woman's Work in a Man's World* (Spradley and Mann 1975). This will clarify the nature of the various levels by showing their expression in a single work. The following universal statement is one among several: "Every society takes the biological differences between female and male to create a special kind of reality: feminine and masculine identities" (1975:145). In the context of a specific bar in a specific city, we made an assertion about a universal feature of human experience.

Level Two: Cross-Cultural Descriptive Statements

The second level of abstraction includes statements about two or more societies, assertions that are true for some societies but not necessarily for all societies. Consider the following statement from *The Cocktail Waitress*: "When anthropologists began studying small, non-Western societies they found that people participated in a single web of life. . . . [W]hen we turn to complex societies such as our own, the number of cultural perspectives for any situation increases radically" (1975: 8, 9). This statement says something about two very large classes of human societies—the small, non-Western ones and the complex ones. Such a descriptive statement helps to convey an understanding of even the most specific place such as Brady's Bar. Cross-cultural descriptive statements help place a cultural scene in the broader picture of human cultures, something every ethnographer is concerned about doing. These kinds of statements say to the reader, "This cultural scene is not merely one little interesting group of people; it is a part of the human species in a particular way. It is like many other cultural scenes, but it is also different from many others." By means of contrast you have conveyed an important dimension of the culture.

Level Three: General Statements about a Society or Cultural Group

This kind of statement appears to be specific, but in fact remains quite general. "The Kwakiutl live in villages along coastal bays" is a general statement about a cultural group. "The Pygmies live in the forest and play musical instruments" is another general statement. We can make such statements about complex societies also: "American culture is based on the value of materialism." Or we can make such statements about recurrent cultural scenes, or groups of people who have learned similar cultural scenes: "Air traffic controllers work under great stress"; "Police departments must gather, classify, and record a great deal of important information."

In our study of Brady's Bar, we included statements at this level; they did not refer exclusively to Brady's Bar, but to all the institutions of which Brady's was one example: "Bars, in general, are places of employment for hundreds of thousands of women, almost always as cocktail waitresses. Their role in bars tends to be an extension of their role at home—serving the needs of men. . . . Like most institutions of American society, men hold sway at the center of social importance" (1975:145).

Level Four: General Statements about a Specific Cultural Scene

When we move down one level of abstraction, we can note many statements about a particular culture or cultural scene. Most ethnographies are filled with statements at this level. "The Fort Rupert Kwakiutl engage in seine fishing." "The air traffic controllers at the Minneapolis International Airport work one of three shifts."

Participant observation provides many statements at this level. We can say things like, "The waitresses at Brady's get hassled by customers" or "Tramps aren't really tramps unless they make the bucket." These are descriptive statements about a particular scene or group, but even so, they are still general in nature. Moreover, even when expressed by an informant and used in an ethnography as a quotation from an informant, they represent an abstraction. Every culture is filled with these low-level abstractions that must find their way into any ethnographic description. Here is an example from Brady's Bar: "At one level, Brady's Bar is primarily a place of business. At another level, Brady's Bar is a place where men can come to play out exaggerated masculine roles, acting out their fantasies of sexual prowess, and reaffirming their own male identities. Brady's Bar is a men's ceremonial center" (1975:130-31).

This level of ethnographic writing contains many of the themes the ethnographer wants to present to the reader. Thus, the theme of males expressing their identities in many different ways—in the way space is organized, the way drinks are ordered, and the like—is described in statements at this level. Sometimes one can encapsulate general statements at Level Four in a quotation from an informant; they still remain statements of a very general nature. Making use of an informant quotation helps provide a sense of immediacy and gives the reader a closer acquaintance with the culture, but we must move to even more specific levels.

Level Five: Specific Statements about a Cultural Domain

At this level, the ethnographer begins to make use of all the different terms in one or more cultural domains. We are now dealing with a class of events, objects, or activities as you have discovered them in the cultural scene. For example, here is an ethnographic statement at this level from my research on the factory that makes tannery equipment: "One of the most important jobs that men do is to make drums. A drum can be small, such as a barrel, or more than thirty feet across. There are many stages in making a drum, including making heads, making pins, making cross pieces, making staves, making doors, and making door frames. The entire process of making a drum can take as long as a week and involve the work of several men."

Descriptive statements at this level can make reference to taxonomies and paradigms that encapsulate a great deal of information. However, these representations in themselves seldom communicate more than a skeleton of relationships to the reader. In order to translate these into a description that will be understood, a great deal of narrative description at this level and the next more specific level is required.

Here is a brief example of a specific statement about the domain, "*asking for a drink,*" which makes up part of the culture of cocktail waitresses. "One frequent way that men ask for a drink is not to ask for a drink at all. In the situation where it is appropriate to ask for a drink, they ask instead for the waitress. This may be done in the form of *teasing, hustling, hassling,* or some other speech act" (1975:132).

Level Six: Specific Incident Statements

In one sense, Levels One through Five all contrast sharply with Level Six, which takes the reader immediately to the actual level of behavior and objects, to the level of perceiving these things. Consider an example from Brady's Bar at this level, closely related to all the examples given at the other five levels of abstraction: "Sandy is working the upper section on Friday night. She walks up to the corner table where there is a group of five she has never seen before: four guys and a girl who are loud and boisterous. She steps up to the table and asks, "Are you ready to order now?" One of the males grabs her by the waist and jerks her towards him. "I already know what I want! I'll take you," he says as he smiles innocently up at her" (1975:132). As a reader, you immediately begin to see things happening, perhaps feel things the actors in this situation feel. Instead of merely being *told* what people know, how they generate behavior from this knowledge, and how they interpret things, you have been *shown* this cultural knowledge in action. A good ethnographic translation shows; a poor one only tells.

Perhaps another example of the six levels in ethnographic writing will clarify the effect on the reader. Drawing from my research among tramps, the following statements all describe a single aspect of their experience: begging, borrowing, panhandling, lending, and otherwise exchanging things.

LEVEL ONE: Reciprocity among human beings is balanced where two people give to each other over time, each giving and each receiving. Such reciprocity occurs in all societies.

LEVEL TWO: Tramps, like those who live in tribal villages, depend on one another in time of need. They expect others to reciprocate. A Kwakiutl Indian will give in a potlatch and later receive gifts at someone else's potlatch. A tramp will give to another tramp and also beg from another tramp.

LEVEL THREE: Tramps engage in much more reciprocal exchange than do other members of the larger society. This kind of exchange takes many forms.

LEVEL FOUR: A tramp in the Seattle City Jail will exchange goods and services with other tramps. If he is a trusty in the jail, he might exchange a service for money with someone in lockup.

LEVEL FIVE: (*Informant's statement*) "Yes, a tramp will beg from other tramps. If you're panhandling you can expect another tramp to give you money or a cigarette if he has it. You realize that sometime he will need something and then it will be your turn."

LEVEL SIX: It was a dull Tuesday afternoon and a slight mist of rain was blowing gently in from the Puget Sound. Joe had become a kickout an hour earlier; several minutes ago he walked off the elevator on the first floor of the Public Safety Building and found his way to the street. Pulling the collar of his worn tweed jacket up around his neck, he hunched his shoulders slightly and headed downtown, wondering where he would find money for a drink or even a cigarette. He might have to make a flop under the bridge on Washington Street tonight to stay out of the rain. He saw a man approaching him as he headed slowly down James Street, obviously another tramp. Looked like a home guard tramp, but he couldn't tell for sure. "Can you spare a quarter for a jug?" he asked. "I just got a kickout." "No, I'm flat on my ass myself," the other man said, "but how about a smoke, all I got are Bull Durhams." After taking a light too, Joe started on down James Street looking for a tourist or businessman to panhandle.

Ethnographic writing includes statements at all six levels on the continuum from the general to the particular. Effective writing, that which serves to communicate the meanings of a culture to the reader, is achieved by making all these statements, but doing so in a certain *proportion*. Professional journals, in which the author writes primarily for colleagues, tend to consist of statements at Levels One and Two; that is, the description is made in general terms, the author avoiding specific incidents. Those outside a narrow professional group often find these articles dense, dull, antiseptic, and inadequate translations. Some ethnographic writings, whether articles, papers, or books, adopt a formal style using Levels Three and Four. Most dissertations and theses are written at these middle levels of abstraction, although they may contain a great deal of information also at Level Five. They tend to present the bare bones, the skeleton of knowledge, without the flesh of examples and specific incident statements of Level Six. At the other extreme, some ethnographic novels and personal accounts consist entirely of statements at Level Six, with, perhaps, a few statements from Level Five thrown in now and then. This kind of writing holds the reader's attention but may fail to communicate the overall structure of a culture or the nature of ethnography.

It should be clear that mixing the various levels in the desirable proportion depends on the goals of the ethnographer. In *You Owe Yourself a Drunk: An Ethnography of Urban Nomads* (1970), I made a great deal of use of Levels Three through Six, ranging back and forth among statements about tramps generally, to specific incidents. Many of the incidents were contained in quotations from informants. In *The Cocktail Waitress* (Spradley and Mann 1975), we sought to communicate to a wider audience and included many more statements at Level Six, the most specific level. We also tried to relate the culture of Brady's Bar to the universal level of writing more frequently. In retrospect, we tended to scale down the middle level of generalizations. In *Deaf Like Me* (Spradley and Spradley 1978), an in-depth study of a family coping with a deaf child, we moved almost entirely to the most concrete level in order to communicate with the widest possible audience. Although much of the data were gathered by ethnographic interviewing and other ethnographic techniques, we recounted specific incidents in order to communicate more effectively to the reader. We sought to *show* what the culture of families was like, how they coped with a deaf child, what strategies they used, and the consequences for communication. Although statements appear in this study at all the other levels of generalization, they are woven into the particular so thoroughly that they do not stand out. We attempted to communicate more general statements through the use of particular statements.

Each ethnographer will have to determine his or her intended audience. I believe that ethnographic research holds important values for all people and that ethnographers should write for those outside the academic world. I urge students and others to use the middle levels of generalizations sparingly.

Emphasize the most general and the most specific. In ethnographic writing, the concern with the general is incidental to an understanding of the particular for an important reason. It is because generalities are best communicated through particulars. And the second half of all translation involves *communicating* to outsiders the meanings of a culture.

STEPS IN WRITING AN ETHNOGRAPHY

Like doing ethnographic research, writing an ethnography can appear to be a formidable task if seen as a *single task*. All too often, the beginning ethnographer conceives the writing as simply *writing*. You sit down with blank paper and all your fieldnotes and begin writing the ethnography. When it is completed it will require some revision and editing, but the work is largely one long, arduous task.

Underlying the D.R.S. Method of research is the assumption that breaking a large task into smaller ones and placing these in sequence will simplify the work and improve one's performance. This assumption applies equally to writing. However, because each of us has developed patterns of writing from years of experience, it is far more difficult to create a series of steps that have wide applicability. The following steps must be considered as suggestions only. Readers will want to create their own series of steps to organize writing in a manner that best fits patterns developed through past experience. However, the underlying premise, that it is valuable to divide up the writing of an ethnography into tasks, does have wide applicability.

Step One: Select an audience.   Because the audience will influence every aspect of your ethnography, selecting an audience is one of the first things to be done. All writing is an act of communication between human beings and in that sense it is similar to talking. When speaking to someone, there are innumerable cues that remind us that our audience is present. The writer needs to select an audience, identify it clearly, and then keep in mind throughout the writing who that audience is.

When writing for a specific journal or magazine, the ethnographer must carefully scrutinize past issues of the journal to discover the style of writing. You are, in fact, discovering the audience that such a journal is written for. If one intends to write a book-length ethnography, then the audience may be scholars in the field, students, the general public, or some other group.

The best advice I have ever received for selecting an audience came from Marshall Townsend, the editor at the University of Arizona Press:

A basic concept we stress at the University of Arizona Press is that of the "target reader." What we urge YOU as an author to do is to pick out a "target reader" and write in book form for only *one reader*. Pick out some real person *whom you know,* then set down your materials so this person will understand what you are saying. When you have a "target reader," you effect a single level of presentation, rather than trying to provide information to everyone from those who have their doctorates to students in high school who want to delve into the subject just a bit. Choose your level of communication and stay with it—by addressing yourself in your writing to only this one person. We believe you will find this concept a highly workable one.

When you as an author write successfully for one, we as a publisher may be able to take your book and sell thousands of copies because each person feels "this was meant for *me*." On the other hand, if you try to write for thousands, and embrace all of their varied interests and viewpoints, we may not be able to sell a single copy. Stick to your one-level approach, and we as publishers will take care of informing readers at all levels of interest and of understanding how the book will fit into their realm.

Step Two: Select a thesis.   In order to communicate with your audience, you need to have something to say. All too often, ethnographic descriptions appear to be like meandering conversations without a destination. Although of interest to the ethnographer and a few colleagues, such writing will not hold the attention of many more. A thesis is the central message, the point you want to make. There are several sources for finding a thesis.

First, the major themes you have discovered in ethnographic research represent possible theses. For example, a major theme in the culture of tramps was that being in jail affected one's identity, even made a man want to go out and get drunk. In jail a man learned to "hustle," and this reinforced his identity as a tramp trying to "make it" on the street. This theme became the thesis of the ethnography: that jailing drunks, rather than being therapeutic, actually played an important role in creating the identity of tramp. This thesis was summed up in the title of the ethnography, which came from an informant who said, "After thirty days in jail, *you owe yourself a drunk!*"

Second, a thesis for your ethnography may come from the overall goals of ethnography. You may, for example, state your thesis in the following way: "To most people, a bar is a place to drink. But to the cocktail waitress, it is much more complex. It is a world of varied cultural meaning that she learns in order to carry out her work and cope with difficulties. In this paper I want to show just how complex the cultural knowledge of the cocktail waitress is, in contrast to the casual impressions of the outsider." Your thesis can simply be to show that cultural meaning systems are much more complex than we usually think.

Another way to formulate this type of thesis is in terms of a set of recipes for behavior. Culture can be viewed as a set of instructions for carrying out life's ordinary activities. Your thesis would be to show the reader the recipe for being a tramp, a cocktail waitress, or some other kind of person. Frake, in a series of articles, has made effective use of this kind of thesis. For example, he has written on "How to ask for a drink" (1964c) and "How to enter a house" among the Yakan in the Philippines (1975).

Still another way to formulate this type of thesis is to show the tacit rules for behavior. This thesis argues that much goes on in social life that we do not see, that there are tacit rules of behavior that people have learned but seldom discuss. The point of your paper is to make those tacit rules explicit.

Third, a thesis may come from the literature of the social sciences. In one paper on tramps I reviewed the literature on the concept of "reciprocity." Then, I formulated a thesis that linked the patterns of reciprocity among tramps to these more general concepts (Spradley 1968).

When a thesis has been selected, it is useful to state it briefly, perhaps in a single sentence, and place it before you as a constant reminder as you write. This will help organize your paper and integrate it around a single major idea. It will also help the reader to grasp the meanings of the culture in a way that a simple listing of domains and their meanings will not.

Step Three: Make a list of topics and create an outline. Any ethnography will necessarily deal with only selected aspects of a culture. Furthermore, you will use only part of the material you have collected. This step involves reviewing your fieldnotes and the cultural inventory you made and listing topics you think should be included in the final description. Some of these topics will be things like "introduction" and "conclusion." Once listed, you can then make an outline based around your thesis. This will divide up your actual writing into sections, each of which can be done as a separate unit. If you have been writing short descriptive pieces throughout the project (See Appendix B), many or all of these may fit into the outline.

Step Four: Write a rough draft of each section. A rough draft is intended to be rough, unfinished, unpolished. One of the great roadblocks for many writers is the desire to revise each sentence as it goes down on paper. Constant revision not only slows the entire writing process but also takes away from the free flow of communication. Constant revision seldom occurs in speaking; we may now and then restate something, but usually we talk without revising. *Write as you talk* is an excellent rule to follow in composing a rough draft of each section.

Step Five: Revise the outline and create subheads. Almost always the outline from which one writes becomes changed in the process of writing. Once a rough draft is completed for each section, it is a good idea to make a new outline, rearranging sections as appropriate. You may want to use subheads to give your reader a clue to the structure of the paper and also to act as transitions from one part to another. Native folk terms can often be used as subheads in an ethnography, helping to create a view that reflects the cultural knowledge of your informants.

Step Six: Edit the rough draft. At this point in the writing you will have a rough draft of your paper, a fairly clear outline, and a number of subheadings you want to use throughout the paper. Now it is time to go over it with an eye to improving the details of writing. Work through each section and at the same time keep the entire description in mind. Make changes directly on the pages you had previously written. When you want to add a paragraph or sentence, write them on the back of the page or on a separate piece of paper with instructions as to where they will appear. At this stage, it is often useful to ask a friend to read over the manuscript and make general comments. An outside perspective is especially useful for making improvements that will enhance the communicative power of the description.

Step Seven: Write the introduction and conclusion. By now the description has taken on substantial form and you can write these two parts of the paper in a more effective manner. Some writers find that they write better if they write a rough introduction at the start of the writing but save the conclusion until the end. In either case, now is the time to review both the introduction and conclusion and revise them to fit the paper.

Step Eight: Reread your manuscript for examples. Examples involve writing at the lowest level of abstraction. Because of their importance in communication, a special reading of the paper to see if you have used enough examples is highly desirable. Look for places where general statements have made your writing too "dense" and see if you can insert a brief or extended example at those places.

Step Nine: Write the final draft. In some cases this will merely involve typing the paper or turning it over to someone else to type. In other cases, you will need to go carefully over the manuscript again, making the final editorial changes. Using steps such as this means you have been over the entire manuscript numerous times during the course of writing. Instead of a single, first-draft-as-final-draft, your paper has gone through a series of developmental stages.

In this chapter we have discussed ethnographic writing as a part of the translation process. Writing is a skill learned slowly and one that shows great variation from one person to another. The suggestions in this chapter are offered only as general guidelines, not as hard-and-fast rules that every writer should try to follow.

Tasks

12.1 Write a rough draft of an ethnography.
12.2 Conduct additional research as needed to fill gaps in your data.
12.3 Write a final draft of an ethnography.

APPENDICES

Appendix A
The Developmental Research Sequence Method

This book has grown out of an attempt to develop a more systematic approach to anthropological fieldwork. I call that approach the Developmental Research Sequence (D.R.S.) Method. My interest began with a rather simple observation: *some tasks are best accomplished before other tasks when undertaking ethnographic fieldwork*. Ethnographers cannot do everything at once, even though fieldwork sometimes appears to demand it. Participant observation, the field technique presented in this book, involves a series of tasks best carried out in some kind of *sequence*. The ethnographer, for example, must locate a social situation before making observations; some observations are best made before others; taking fieldnotes must precede analysis of data. Ethnographic interviews also involve a sequence of fieldwork tasks; that sequence is presented in *The Ethnographic Interview* (Spradley 1979).

As I began to work with this idea of *sequenced* tasks, I found that it had two applications. First, it helped guide my own ethnographic research. Second, in consulting with professional ethnographers, graduate students in several disciplines, and also undergraduate students, use of the D.R.S. Method helped solve many fieldwork problems. With my colleague David McCurdy I used this approach in numerous undergraduate courses on ethnographic interviewing at Macalester College. With Jeff Nash, Associate Professor of Sociology at Macalester College, I taught a course based on participant observation where many of these ideas were originally developed. In 1976-77, through a Chautauqua-type short course sponsored by A.A.A.S., I presented many of these ideas to professionals from anthropology, sociology, psychology, education, and political science who were interested in ethnographic research. Many of them made use of this approach in their own research and teaching and their ideas have helped refine and clarify what is presented here.

Traditionally, anthropologists have learned to do fieldwork toward the end of their professional training. Frequently, as in my own case, it has meant a kind of sink-or-swim experience. After years of listening to lectures, reading journals, and writing library research papers, the ethnographer arrived in some strange community where people spoke an alien language. The goal was clear: *to discover the cultural patterns that made life meaningful to these people*. The field techniques were also clear: *interviewing and participant observation*. But we only vaguely understood the way to actually conduct ethnographic interviews or engage in participant observation. The traditional ethnographer, while knowing a great deal *about* other cultures, often did not have systematic training in how to make original discoveries from the people themselves. The skills for doing ethnography had to be learned in the field in a hit-or-miss fashion.

And so the ethnographer started hanging around, watching, listening, and writing things down. Those who seemed willing or talkative became key informants. In a few months, the stack of fieldnotes about what people said and did grew quite large. Through trial and error, through persistence and patience, most ethnographers somehow learned to do rather good ethnography. They stayed in the field for six months, a year, eighteen months. They found out a great deal about the culture, worrying now and then if they had missed some important area of life.

The fieldwork period drew to a close and the ethnographer returned home with notebooks filled with observations and interpretations. Sorting through fieldnotes in the months that followed, most ethnographers discovered questions they should have asked, important lines of inquiry they should have followed. But even with many gaps in the notes, the ethnographer compared, contrasted, analyzed, synthesized, and wrote. And rewrote. The end was in sight: an ethnographic description that translated an alien way of life into terms that others could understand. By the end of the project, one had finally learned to do ethnography—*by doing it*.

The Developmental Research Sequence approach shares a common feature with this traditional way of learning to do fieldwork. Both rest on the assumption that the best way to learn to do ethnography is by doing it. This is reflected in Part Two of this book which consists of specific tasks arranged in sequential order. Part One, "Ethnographic Research," can be read quickly to review some basic concepts related to doing fieldwork, but Part Two, "The Developmental Research Sequence," requires a different approach. Each step begins with a statement of D.R.S. objectives—what one must learn by doing before proceeding to the next step. After a discussion of concepts and techniques, each step ends with a list of D.R.S. tasks required for doing fieldwork. Many of the later steps in the sequence only make sense *after* one has gained at least minimal experience in doing participant observation. Although this book is designed for the person seeking to acquire some skill in participant observation, I believe it will also be of value to the experienced ethnographer. In the latter case, the sequence of steps must be adapted to what one has found works best from previous experience in the field.

The five principles that underly the D.R.S. Method of learning and doing ethnography form the basis for the way this book is organized, for the inclusion of some ideas and the omission of others. My goal is not to survey the professional literature on participant observation, but rather to provide a workable approach to learning this field technique for doing ethnography.

1. The Single-Technique Principle. The D.R.S. Method makes a distinction among ethnographic techniques and selects one for learning purposes.

In order to describe another culture, ethnographers use many techniques. They act as participant observers, recording what people do and say in the course of ordinary activities. They observe ceremonies and work activities such as fishing and building houses. They make casual inquiries as they follow people around watching what they do. They record life histories to discover how individuals experience their culture. They record folk tales and legends. They conduct ethnographic interviews with key informants, carefully analyzing responses to questions. They record genealogies. They may use projective tests. In the field, the experienced ethnographer may pursue all of these approaches at the same time. However, for purposes of *learning* to do ethnography, it is best to focus on mastering one technique at a time. This book deals only with participant observation, not because it is the best source of data, but because it is one indispensable technique for doing ethnography.

2. The Task Identification Principle. The D.R.S. Method identifies the basic tasks and specific objectives required by a particular field technique. In this book I have identified twelve major tasks. When a person carries out these tasks, two things occur. First, one learns the basic skills of participant observation and writing a cultural description. Second, one carries out original research on a particular cultural scene.

3. The Developmental Sequence Principle. The D.R.S. Method is based on a developmental sequence of specific tasks necessary to complete each of the major steps. The sequenced nature of the assignments helps to *focus* ethnographic research. The ethnographer in the field is confronted with hundreds of things that could be studied. Even in a single interview there are many possible ways to go. The sequenced nature of the steps does two things: (a) it enables a person to improve basic research skills in a systematic manner, and (b) it allows one to study a cultural scene in a way that is efficient and workable. This will lead to a rapid growth in research competence, a sense of control, and reduction in the anxiety of fieldwork.

4. The Original Research Principle. The D.R.S. Method takes a person through to the completion of an original ethnographic research project. The steps in Part Two of this book are *not* merely training exercises. They represent steps in carrying out original research. Because of this goal, the Developmental Research Sequence covers, in addition to observation skills, techniques for analysis of fieldnotes, suggestions for organizing a cultural description based on participant observation, and specific guidelines for writing the final ethnographic description.

I have known a number of graduate and undergraduate students who have published their research which resulted from following the D.R.S. Method. Others have read their papers at professional meetings, and many continue their projects or shift from participant observation to ethnographic interviews on the same cultural scene. Throughout this book I have drawn examples from the work of professionals and students alike. I refer to all of them as *ethnographers*; through their use of the D.R.S. Method, they were engaged in doing original research.

5. The Problem-Solving Principle.   The D.R.S. Method is based on the problem-solving process. Every ethnographer knows that fieldwork presents an endless series of problems. In one way or another, the successful ethnographer must become a successful problem solver. Part of the excitement of doing fieldwork comes from the challenge of problem solving, a process involving six steps: (1) define the problem, (2) identify possible causes, (3) consider possible solutions, (4) select the best solution, (5) carry out your plan, and (6) evaluate the results.

The objectives and tasks presented in each of the twelve steps were developed by applying this problem-solving process to participant observation and ethnographic writing. From my own experience, from talking with other professional ethnographers, and from the experiences of hundreds of students, certain recurrent problems became apparent. Some were *fieldwork problems*: cancelled appointments, unwillingness to answer questions, suspicion, failure to gain rapport. *Conceptual problems* arose from lack of understanding of fundamental concepts related to doing ethnography. *Analysis problems* came from not knowing what to do with the raw information gathered from participant observation. *Writing problems* included organizing the final report and knowing what to include as well as how to go about the task of writing. The sequence of objectives and tasks throughout the twelve steps anticipates all of these problems as well as others. The concepts, objectives, tasks, and examples in each step arose, in part, from applying the problem-solving process to the most common difficulties in doing participant observation.

However, every fieldwork project is unique and presents new problems. For this reason, the ethnographer must apply the problem-solving process throughout a research project. I encourage beginning ethnographers to make a systematic effort to do this, monitoring their progress, identifying problems, developing lists of possible solutions, selecting the best ones, carrying them out, and evaluating the results.

Working in a group can often facilitate the application of the problem-solving process to ethnographic fieldwork. In both graduate and undergraduate classes I have scheduled a weekly problem-solving laboratory, which begins with my asking for difficulties encountered during the previous week of research. The first statement of a problem usually needs to be refined. Once the group has clearly defined the problem, we try to generate as many solutions as possible. From this list, we can discuss the best solutions and how to carry them out. Sometimes students meet in small groups of four or five and use the problem-solving process to work through their current difficulties or evaluate the success of carrying out a solution.

Appendix B
Developmental Research Sequence Writing Tasks

In completing each step in the D.R.S. Method, it is useful to do some writing. Beginning to write early will result in rough draft material that can find its way into the final ethnography. Of course, you will be writing field-notes, a journal, and interpretations that suggest themselves. Also, each of the assignments involves some writing. The tasks outlined here are designed specifically with the final written ethnography in mind. Writing two to four pages each week about topics that may fit into the final report will influence your research. These projects will stimulate you to make certain kinds of analyses and continually think about the end product of the research. These topics are *suggestions*; you may want to follow some or all of them, or design specific writing that fits more directly your own research.

1. Locating a Social Situation

The nature of ethnographic research. One cannot assume that the reader of an ethnographic description will understand the nature of the investigation. Write a brief statement that tells the reader what an ethnography is. Identify and define key concepts such as culture, ethnography, participant observation, and social situation. Illustrate these concepts from your own experience. Several pages about the nature of ethnography may serve as an introduction to the final report and will certainly help to clarify the concepts as you begin research.

2. Doing Participant Observation

The role of language in ethnographic research. Discuss briefly the role of language in all phases of ethnographic research. Discuss how the participant observer's own language influences the data.

3. Making an Ethnographic Record

Beginning an ethnographic research project. Describe for a reader how you started ethnographic research. Write in the first person to test that style as one option for the final ethnography. Include details on how you made the decision to select the cultural scene, how you located a social situation and what took place when you started observing. Include your own reactions to this early phase of fieldwork.

4. Making Descriptive Observations

The physical setting. Describe the physical setting of the social situation. Base your writing on observations made during fieldwork. Begin by making a list of specific locales and objects. This writing task will make use of your first impressions before they fade and also bring to light needed information.

5. Making a Domain Analysis

Summary of the cultural scene. Write a preliminary overview of the cultural scene on the basis of the domains you have identified in your preliminary search. Write in broad terms to describe the total scene, or what you know about it.

6. Making Focused Observations

Revise the summary of the cultural scene. Rewrite the paper you wrote for Step Five, adding important domains, revising the style into a coherent but brief overview of the cultural scene.

7. Making a Taxonomic Analysis

Describe a cultural domain. Select a set of terms that make up one domain or are part of a larger domain and write a description of it.

8. Making Selected Observations

Write a dialogue on a cultural domain. Select a domain you have analyzed and create a meaningful dialogue between two people who know the culture. Describe the situation in which they are communicating. This form of writing will enable you to experiment with a slightly different style.

9. Making a Componential Analysis

Describe a cultural domain. Select a different cultural domain and write a formal description of that domain, making clear the meaning of terms and their relationships. Give specific examples to show some of the attributes that reveal contrasts among the terms.

10. Discovering Cultural Themes

Describe a cultural theme. Select one or more cultural themes and write a brief paper that shows how the theme connects several domains of the culture.

11. Taking a Cultural Inventory

Describe the development of your research. Describe the overall cause of your investigation. Include a discussion of ethical problems that have arisen and how these have been solved.

12. Writing an Ethnography

Suggestions for future research. Write a brief paper that identifies several of the most important areas for future research on the cultural scene in light of your discoveries. What would you study if you had more time or recommended that someone else study in this scene?

BIBLIOGRAPHY

AGAR, MICHAEL
1973 *Ripping and Running: A Formal Ethnography of Urban Heroin Addicts.*
New York: Seminar Press.
1976 "Themes revisited: some problems in cognitive anthropology." Unpublished paper, Department of Anthropology, University of Houston.

BEAN, SUSAN S.
1976 "Soap operas: sagas of American kinship," in *The American Dimension.*
Port Washington, N.Y.: Alfred.

BECKER, H. S.
1963 *Outsiders.* New York: Free Press.

BENEDICT, RUTH
1934 *Patterns of Culture.* New York: Houghton Mifflin.

BLACK, MARY, AND DUANE METZGER
1964 "Ethnographic description and the study of law," in *The Ethnography of Law,* Laura Nader, ed. *American Anthropologist* 67(2):141-65.

BLUMER, HERBERT
1969 *Symbolic Interactionism.* Englewood Cliffs, N.J.: Prentice-Hall.

BOAS, FRANZ
1966 *Kwakiutl Ethnography* (edited by Helen Codere). Chicago: University of Chicago Press.

CARLSON, KATHERINE
1977 "Reciprocity in the marketplace: tipping in an urban nightclub," in *Conformity and Conflict: Readings in Cultural Anthropology,* 3rd ed. James P. Spradley and David W. McCurdy, eds., pp. 337-47. Boston: Little, Brown.

D'ANDRADE, ROY
1976 "A propositional analysis of U.S. American beliefs about illness," in *Meaning in Anthropology,* Keith Basso and Henry A. Selby, eds., pp. 155-80. Albuquerque: University of New Mexico Press.

DEVNEY, ROBERT
1974 "The health and social culture of quadriplegics." B.A. Honors Thesis, Department of Anthropology, Macalester College, St. Paul, Minn.

DIXON, CAROL
1972 "Guided options as a pattern of control in a headstart program." *Urban Life and Culture* 1:203-16.

EDGERTON, ROBERT
1978 *On the Beach.* Berkeley: University of California Press.

EHRMAN, SUZI
1977 "The lord of the rings: ethnography of a directory assistance telephone operator." Unpublished seminar paper, Department of Anthropology, Macalester College, St. Paul, Minn.
1978 "Airport '78: the waiting public: ethnography of killing time in the airport." Unpublished paper, Department of Anthropology, Macalester College, St. Paul, Minn.

BIBLIOGRAPHY

ESTENSON, JOAN
    1978   "Picketers and arsonists: an ethnography of opposition to an abortion clinic." Unpublished paper, Department of Anthropology, Macalester College, St. Paul, Minn.

FERRY, DAVID
    1978   "I think that this would be easier with a machine: an ethnography of waiting in line." Unpublished paper, Department of Anthropology, Macalester College, St. Paul, Minn.

FRAKE, CHARLES O.
    1964a "Notes on queries in ethnography." *American Anthropologist* 66(3), Part 2:132-45.
    1964b "A structural description of Subanun religious behavior," in *Explorations in Cultural Anthropology,* Ward Goodenough, ed., pp. 111-30. New York: Mc Graw-Hill.
    1964c "How to ask for a drink in Subanun." *American Anthropologist* 66(2):127-32.
    1975   "How to enter a Yakan house," in *Sociocultural Dimensions of Language Use,* Mary Sanchez and Ben Blount, eds., pp. 25-40. New York: Academic Press.
    1977   "Plying frames can be dangerous: some reflections on methodology in cognitive anthropology." *Quarterly Newsletter of the Institute for Comparative Human Development* 3:1-7. New York: Rockefeller University.

FRANK, PEGGY
    1976   "How to cross the urban no man's land." Unpublished paper, Department of Anthropology, Macalester College, St. Paul, Minn.

GLASER, BARNEY G., AND ANSELM L. STRAUSS
    1967   *The Discovery of Grounded Theory: Strategies for Qualitative Research.* Chicago: Aldine.

GOFFMAN, ERVING
    1961   *Asylums.* Garden City, N.Y.: Doubleday.

GORDON, DAVID
    1974   "The Jesus People: an identity synthesis." *Urban Life and Culture* 3:159-78.

HAGSTROM, CATHY
    1978   "It feels good to be recognized in public." Unpublished paper, Department of Anthropology, Macalester College, St. Paul, Minn.

HALL, EDWARD T.
    1959   *The Silent Language.* Garden City, N.Y.: Doubleday.
    1966   *The Hidden Dimension.* Garden City, N.Y.: Doubleday.

HALL, GAIL
    1976   "Workshop of a ballerina: an exercise in professional socialization." *Urban Life and Culture* 6:193-220.

HANSON, JANE
    1978   "At the museum: child handling among Indian artifacts." Unpublished paper, Department of Anthropology, Macalester College, St. Paul, Minn.

HAYANO, DAVID M.
    1978   "Strategies for the management of luck and action in an urban poker parlor." *Urban Life and Culture* 6:475-88.

HENRY, JULES
1963   *Culture Against Man.* New York: Random House.

HICKS, GEORGE L.
1976   *Appalachian Valley.* New York: Holt, Rinehart and Winston.

HYMES, DELL H.
1978   "What is ethnography?" Sociolinguistics Working Paper #45, Southwest Educational Development Laboratory, Austin, Texas.

IRVINE, JUDITH T.
1974   "Strategies of status manipulation in Wolof greeting," in *Explorations in the Ethnography of Speaking,* Richard Bauman and Joel Sherzer, eds., pp. 167-91. New York: Cambridge University Press.

JACOBS, JERRY
1974   *Fun City: An Ethnographic Study of a Retirement Community.* New York: Jerry Jacobs.

JACOBSON, DAVID
1973   *Itinerant Townsmen: Friendship and Social Order in Urban Uganda.* Menlo Park, Calif.: Cummings.

KEISER, LINCOLN
1969   *The Vicelords.* New York: Holt, Rinehart and Winston.

KIEFER, THOMAS M.
1968   "Institutionalized friendship and warfare among the Tausaug of Jolo," *Ethnology* 7:225-44.

KRUFT, JEAN
1978   "A humanitarian cause: an ethnography of selling blood plasma." Unpublished paper, Department of Anthropology, Macalester College, St. Paul, Minn.

KRUSE, LIS-MARIE
1975   "Teenage drinking and sociability." *Urban Life and Culture* 4:54-78.

LE COMPTE, MARGARET
1978   "Learning to work: the hidden curriculum of the classroom." *Anthropology and Education Quarterly* 9:22-37.

LEWIS, OSCAR
1963   *The Children of Sanchez: Autobiography of a Mexican Family.* New York: Vintage.

LIEBOW, ELLIOT
1967   *Tally's Corner.* Boston: Little, Brown.

LOFLAND, JOHN
1976   *Doing Social Life: The Qualitative Study of Human Interaction in Natural Settings.* New York: Wiley.

LYND, ROBERT S.
1939   *Knowledge for What?* Princeton, N.J.: Princeton University Press.

MAISEL, ROBERT
1974   "The flea market as an action scene." *Urban Life and Culture* 2:488-505.

MALINOWSKI, BRONISLAW
1922   *Argonauts of the Western Pacific.* London: Routledge.
1950   *Argonauts of the Western Pacific.* New York: Dutton.

BIBLIOGRAPHY

MANIS, JEROME, AND BERNARD MELTZER, EDS.
1967 *Symbolic Interaction: A Reader in Social Psychology*. Boston: Allyn and Bacon.

MANN, BRENDA
1976 "The ethics of field work in an urban bar," in *Ethics and Anthropology: Dilemmas in Field Work*. Michael Rynkiewich and James Spradley, eds., pp. 95-109. New York: Wiley.

MANN, LEON
1973 "Learning to live with lines," in *Urbanman: The Psychology of Urban Survival*. John Helmer and Neil A. Eddington, eds., pp. 42-61. New York: Free Press.

MC CORD, JOAN, AND WILLIAM MC CORD
1958 "The effects of parental role model on criminality." *Journal of Social Issues* 14:66-75.

MC CURDY, DAVID W.
1971 "The changing economy of an Indian village," in *Conformity and Conflict: Readings in Cultural Anthropology*. James P. Spradley and David W. McCurdy, eds., pp. 219-28. Boston: Little, Brown.

MEGGITT, MERVYN
1974 "Pigs are our hearts!" *Oceania* 44:165-203.

MONSEY, BARBARA
1978 "Vending machines: order and disorder." Unpublished paper, Department of Anthropology, Macalester College, St. Paul, Minn.

NASH, JEFFREY
1975 "Bus riding: community on wheels." *Urban Life and Culture* 4:99-124.
1977 "Decoding the runner's wardrobe," in *Conformity and Conflict: Readings in Cultural Anthropology*, 3rd ed. James P. Spradley and David W. McCurdy, eds., pp. 172-86. Boston: Little, Brown.

NELSON, RICHARD K.
1969 *Hunters of the Northern Ice*. Chicago: University of Chicago Press.

NORTHROP, DAPHNE
1978 "I look better when I prance: an ethnography of track runners." Unpublished paper, Department of Anthropology, Macalester College, St. Paul, Minn.

OPLER, MORRIS E.
1945 "Themes as dynamic forces in culture." *American Journal of Sociology* 53:198-206.

ORBACH, MICHAEL K.
1977 *Hunters, Seamen, and Entrepreneurs*. Berkeley: University of California Press.

READ, KENNETH E.
1965 *The High Valley*. New York: Scribners.

RIEMER, JEFFREY W.
1977 "Varieties of opportunistic research." *Urban Life and Culture* 5:467-78.

ROHLEN, THOMAS P.
1974 *For Harmony and Strength*. Berkeley: University of California Press.

ROTH, JULIUS A.

1963 *Timetables: Structuring the Passage of Time in Hospital Treatment and Other Careers*. New York: Bobbs-Merrill.

RYBSKI, JOHN

1974 "Flying like a butterfly from cloud to cloud: an ethnography of soaring in Minnesota." Unpublished paper, Department of Anthropology, Macalester College, St. Paul, Minn.

SANDERS, WILLIAM B.

1973 "Pinball occasions," in *People in Places: The Sociology of the Familiar*. Arnold Bierenbaum and Edward Sagarin, eds. New York: Praeger.

SINGWI, VEENA

1977 "An ethnography of a soda and grill." Unpublished paper, Department of Anthropology, Macalester College, St. Paul, Minn.

SOLOWAY, IRV, AND JAMES WALTERS

1977 "Workin' the corner: the ethics and legality of ethnographic fieldwork among active heroin addicts," in *Street Ethnography*, Robert S. Weppner, ed., pp. 159-78. Beverly Hills, Calif.: Sage Publications.

SPRADLEY, JAMES P.

1968 "A cognitive analysis of tramp behavior," in *Proceedings of the Eighth International Congress of Anthropological and Ethnological Sciences*. Tokyo: Japan Science Council.

1969 *Guests Never Leave Hungry: The Autobiography of James Sewid, a Kwakiutl Indian*. New Haven: Yale University Press.

1970 *You Owe Yourself a Drunk: An Ethnography of Urban Nomads*. Boston: Little, Brown.

1971 "Beating the drunk charge," in *Conformity and Conflict: Readings in Cultural Anthropology*, James P. Spradley and David W. Mc Curdy, eds., pp. 351-58. Boston: Little, Brown.

1973 "The ethnography of crime in American society," in *Cultural Illness and Health*, Laura Nader and Thomas Maretzki, eds. Anthropological Studies, No. 9. Washington, D.C.: American Anthropological Association.

1976 "The revitalization of American culture: an anthropological perspective," in *Qualities of Life: Critical Choices for Americans*, Vol. III, pp. 99-122. Lexington, Mass.: Heath.

1979 *The Ethnographic Interview*. New York: Holt, Rinehart and Winston.

SPRADLEY, JAMES P., AND BRENDA MANN

1975 *The Cocktail Waitress: Women's Work in a Male World*. New York: Wiley.

SPRADLEY, JAMES P., AND DAVID W. MC CURDY

1971 *Conformity and Conflict: Readings in Cultural Anthropology*. Boston: Little, Brown (2nd ed., 1974; 3rd ed., 1977).

1972 *The Cultural Experience*. Chicago: Science Research Associates.

SPRADLEY, JAMES P., AND ALAN R. SCHROEDL

1972 "The raw and the cooked: an ethnography of communicative competence." Unpublished manuscript, Department of Anthropology, Macalester College, St. Paul, Minn.

SPRADLEY, THOMAS S., AND JAMES P. SPRADLEY

1978 *Deaf Like Me*. New York: Random House.

BIBLIOGRAPHY

STARR, PAUL D.
  1978 "Ethnic categories and identification in Lebanon." *Urban Life and Culture*
  7:111-42.
SUGARMAN, BARRY
  1974 *Daytop Village: A Therapeutic Community*. New York: Holt, Rinehart and
  Winston.
TOLZMANN, BECKY
  1978 "Safety in the arcade: an ethnography on knowing the danger signals in an
  urban setting." Unpublished paper, Department of Anthropology, Macalester College, St. Paul, Minn.
TURNBULL, COLIN
  1961 *The Forest People*. New York: Simon and Schuster.
VERIN, NINA
  1978 "Deaf and hearing: ethnography of a mainstreamed classroom." Unpublished paper, Department of Anthropology, Macalester College, St. Paul,
  Minn.
WALUM, LAUREL RICHARDSON
  1974 "The changing door ceremony: notes on the operation of sex roles." *Urban
  Life and Culture* 2:506-15.
WARD, BARBARA
  1966 *Spaceship Earth*. New York: Columbia University Press.
WHITING, JOHN, I. CHILD, AND W. LAMBERT
  1966 *Field Guide for a Study of Socialization*. New York: Wiley.
WOLCOTT, HARRY F.
  1967 *A Kwakiutl Village and School*. New York: Holt, Rinehart and Winston.

INDEX

accessibility, as criterion for selecting social situation, 47–48
act, as dimension of social situation, 78, 82–83, 102
active participation, 60–61
activities
as dimension of social situation, 41–42, 43, 78, 82–83, 86, 102
recurrent, as criterion for selection of social situation, 50
actors, as dimension of social situation, 39, 41, 43, 78, 82–83, 86, 102
Agar, Michael, 143, 149
alternative realities, 14, 16
amalgamated language, 68
American Anthropological Association, 20, 25
American culture, 15–16, 18–19, 29
analysis notes, 72
analysis problems, 178
analytic domains, 91, 109, 110, 111
analytic terms, 90, 91, 115
replacement of, by folk terms, 124
analyzed domains, 156–157
Apache, 140–141
Appalachia, 3–4, 7, 29
attributes, 131–132, 137, 139
definition of, 131
audience, ethnographer's, 167, 168–169

bank culture, 47
Bean, Susan S., 59
Becker, H. S., 61
Benedict, Ruth, 141, 142
biculturalism, 15
Black, Mary, 32
Blumer, Herbert, 8, 9
Boas, Franz, 29

card-sorting contrast questions, 126–127
Carlson, Katherine, 153
Child, I., 31
Cocktail Waitress: Woman's Work in a Man's World, The (Spradley and Mann), 163, 167
cocktail waitresses, 21, 22, 105, 142, 144, 147, 152–153, 165

cognitive map, culture as, 9
cognitive principle, 141–142, 144
complete participation, 61–62
complex societies
informants in, 21
understanding, 15–16
componential analysis, 34, 87, 129, 130–139, 145–147, 148, 181
definition of, 131
steps in making, 133–139
comprehensive ethnography, 31
conceptual problems, 178
concrete principle, 65, 68–69, 70
condensed account, 69–70
Conformity and Conflict: Readings in Cultural Anthropology, 161
contrast questions, 32, 125–128, 129, 134, 137
card-sorting, 126–127
and dimensions of contrast, 127–128
dyadic, 125–126
in ethnographic interview, 123, 124
triadic, 126
corporations, 19
cover terms, 90, 91, 93, 94, 95, 115, 117, 119, 145–147
definition of, 89
and general cultural domains, 102, 105
cross-cultural comparisons, 13
cross-cultural descriptive statements, 163, 167
cultural anthropology, ethnographic fieldwork as hallmark of, 3
cultural artifacts, 7, 10, 85
definition of, 5–6
cultural behavior, 7, 10, 85
definition of, 5
patterns of, 59–60
cultural complexity, 100
cultural contradictions, as universal cultural themes, 152
cultural deprivation, theory of, 14, 15
cultural description, 10, 140
as central task of ethnography, 13
cultural differences, explanation of, 13
cultural domains, 87, 88–91, 142, 181
in componential analysis, 133–134, 139

189